ALMOST

Who God Is,
What God Does,
and How God
Redeemed the
Life of an Average
Underdog

GUSTAVO CROCKER

THE FOUNDRY
PUBLISHING*

Copyright © 2021 by Gustavo Crocker
The Foundry Publishing®
PO Box 419527
Kansas City, MO 64141
thefoundrypublishing.com

978-0-8341-4049-3

Printed in the
United States of America

Cover Design: J.R. Caines
Interior Design: Sharon Page

Library of Congress Cataloging-in-Publication Data
A complete catalog record for this book is available from the Library of Congress.

The internet addresses, email addresses, and phone numbers in this book are accurate at the time of publication. They are provided as a resource. The Foundry Publishing does not endorse them or vouch for their content or permanence.

10 9 8 7 6 5 4 3 2 1

CONTENTS

PREFACE

San Jerónimo is a small town in rural Guatemala. Even with all the growth of the cities and road systems, the town remains small and rural. In the early colonial times of the 1600s, it was the seat of the Dominican priests in the Verapaz area of the country, but it never developed. Even now, the town has only one main street that is intersected by small alleys and rural paths that remind us of the times when people used ox-pulled carts and horses. San Jerónimo is the town where I was born.

My father was a telegrapher and my mother a seamstress. They moved to San Jerónimo in the 1950s because of my father's job. They were from the predominantly mestizo eastern part of the country but didn't have the means to stay there, so they migrated to a new town that, centuries after Spanish colonization, retained the flavor of the colonial towns with a mixture of Mayan ancestry, African slaves, and *mestizo* Hispanics.[1]

Like many things in life, poverty was somehow relative. My parents were not considered poor because Dad was a civil servant with a steady source of income, and Mom had a trade. They were able

---

1. The term *mestizo* means "mixed" in Spanish. It is generally used throughout Latin America to describe people of mixed race, especially those of European/Spanish and indigenous ancestry.

to afford the basic needs at home, except that the small town didn't have the ways and means for people to emerge out of their poverty and social limitations. There was a small elementary school in town but no secondary schools. Students who wanted to go beyond sixth grade had to be sent to expensive boarding schools, hours away from home. There was a small, basic clinic with no doctor and no medications. The closest hospital was two hours away by bus—a bus that ran twice a day through the dusty roads that connected San Jerónimo with Salamá.

I grew up in that context. I never knew that I was poor, even though I never had access to the things that most children now consider normal. My life was an interesting paradox of having while lacking and lacking while having.

Fast forward to January 1993. My wife, Rachel, and I were serving in Ecuador. Rachel had to have surgery on her ankle because of an old injury. By now we were a couple of young missionaries with two small daughters, learning the ropes of life in the mission field. Since part of my assignment was to train global leaders for the social ministries of the church, I had to travel around the world while my family stayed home under the capable care of my wife. This time, however, someone needed to care for Rachel because I was scheduled to travel to India for an entire month. My mother volunteered to come. She had neither the time nor the money, but she came anyway because helping was in her DNA.

During that visit, my mom met Louie Bustle, who was at that time the director of the mission for our church family in South America. Ever the hostess, my mother had invited the Bustles to share with us a simple Guatemalan meal. (I need to digress here because those simple Guatemalan meals with black beans, cheese, corn tortillas, and grilled steak are the closest thing to the wedding banquet of the Lamb!).

After the meal, Louie asked my mom a question that was obviously meant to stoke her pride: "What do you think about your son, who is not even thirty years old and has worked in nearly fifty countries?"

My mother answered simply and humbly: "I gave this child to the Lord when he was weeks old, and it has been the Lord's business ever since."

I pondered her answer the rest of the evening but waited until our guests had departed before asking her to explain. "Mom," I said, "What did you mean when you said that you gave me to the Lord when I was weeks old and it has been the Lord's business ever since?"

The following biographical sketches may offer some answers.

• • •

A Note about the Cover

There is a story behind the picture that appears on the cover. The person who took the picture was Stanley Storey, a missionary to Guatemala in the early 1960s. He baptized my parents and asked Rev. Federico Guillermo to pray for them. In the Church of the Nazarene, Rev. Guillermo was the first district superintendent ever from a country outside of Home Missions.

When Stan retired in 1992, I was working for Nazarene Compassionate Ministries, and we gave him a copy of the picture framed on Guatemalan wood. He said to me: "You are in the picture. I have spent thirty-five years of my life in your country, and now I pray that you will spend your life in at least thirty-five countries." Twelve years later, I was elected regional director, overseeing the missionary work in more than thirty-six countries.

While my parents were the product of the missionary work of my church, this picture frames the first-ever indigenous judicatory of the church in mission fields, praying for a young couple of converts. In the mother's arms is a sickly child who one day became the first Hispanic person elected to lead a global denomination.

I am humbled to take part in God's plans.

ALMOST ABORTED

I AM THE YOUNGEST of eight children. During the 1960s in rural Guatemala, family planning was either unknown or taboo. From the beginning of their union, Mom and Dad had children like clockwork: one child every two years. Whenever my siblings and I need to remember one another's ages, we just think about our own age and add or subtract the years in multiples of two.

After sibling number seven was born with the assistance of the local midwife, my mom heard about the women's wellness clinic in the department's capital city of Salamá (Guatemalan departments are sort of like U.S. states), and she decided to visit the doctor there. Carrying her newborn baby, Mom went to the doctor for a checkup.

It was, perhaps, the first of her life because all her previous pregnancies and deliveries had been supervised by the town's midwife.

"You gotta stop having children," the doctor told her. "It is irresponsible to have so many children in an environment surrounded by poverty, scarcity, and limitation." Mom and Dad didn't know any different. According to my mother, their only understanding of family planning was the ancestral tradition in the village that nursing your babies would delay pregnancies.

While Mom agreed with the doctor's assessment that having more children would make them even poorer, she also knew it would be difficult to broach the subject with Dad. The cultural norm for all the men in the countryside, regardless of religious belief, was for men to demonstrate their manhood by having children. Nevertheless, Mom took a chance. She decided that she had to do *something* in order to give her seven children better opportunities to make it in the world with their limited family resources. So she agreed to continue seeing the doctor.

After several extensive and expensive visits to Salamá to see the doctor, he decided she would benefit from the family-planning policies and practices the government was implementing in the rural areas of Guatemala. At that time, they were testing the insertion of a T-shaped, copper-plated intrauterine device (IUD). Today, most IUDs are considered medically safe, and their function is to prevent conception, not abort pregnancies. But there have been cases where the device did not work as intended, and any woman who manages to become pregnant while using an IUD will face risks to her health and her pregnancy. Mom felt that she had done her part to help with the family welfare and the future of her seven children. What she didn't know was that these IUDs were still in the experimental phase and would not be deemed safe until 1967—a few years after she had hers implanted.

One day, it happened exactly like clockwork. Just like with the two preceding children born in July, Mom started having the same symptoms she'd had with numbers five, six, and seven. She had stopped nursing them when they were one year old and then, three months later, she was pregnant again! So imagine her surprise when she experienced the signs and symptoms of pregnancy once again after she stopped nursing number seven. How could that happen when IUDs were supposed to be more than 99-percent effective? Was this a different kind of gynecological disease that mirrored a pregnancy but was caused by "the T" (as Mom called her IUD)? The only way to know was to travel the long, dusty road to Salamá to visit the doctor.

"This is bad," said the doctor when my mom explained her situation and he examined her. "You are pregnant *in spite* of the IUD. The worst thing is that the copper in the device has undoubtedly damaged the fetus. You must abort it! This child, if born, will break your coffers and demand your full attention and all of your time and money. If this child even lives, he or she will be disabled with limited mental capacities and damaged organs. You will bear a great burden in your already difficult life. Furthermore, you run the risk of losing your own life while giving birth to a child who may not even live. We must schedule you for an emergency abortion. Go home, leave your one-year-old there, and return alone for the procedure."

The doctor's argument was compelling. Thousands of women have been moved to terminate unplanned pregnancies with less persuasion. Not my mom, however.

The return trip to San Jerónimo was long and torturous. This thirty-three-year-old young mother with a family of seven kids living in poverty now had to decide whether to terminate a life that, according to science and medical knowledge, was going to be an aberration at best, and a risk to her life at worst. On one hand, the doctor's argument made sense. This child could add further financial pressure to her already poor family. On the other hand, she was a Christian, and she knew that God's plans do not always make sense to humanity. She was also convinced that life is a gift from God and that nobody has authority over anyone else's life—not even our own.

11

When she arrived home after her long journey, Mom talked things over with Dad, and together they decided to keep the baby—no matter the cost, no matter the consequences, no matter the risk. Her pregnancy was difficult, made even harder because of the uncertainty of the child's health at birth.

Nevertheless, on the sunny afternoon of Tuesday, July 27, 1963, while my family went through the routine they had grown accustomed to after seven deliveries, I was born. I was small and skinny, delivered with minimal effort and no risk for my mom. And, to the midwife's amusement, I was born "with a cross stuck to his skull." I still have a small dent on my head, from the mark that a T-shaped, copper device left while I fought for my life "from the very moment of conception."

I heard this story for the first time after that dinner in Ecuador in 1993. I asked my mother what went through her mind when she was told by the doctor to abort me because I would represent a risk to her life and the family budget. "You either believe that God is God—or you don't," she said humbly but emphatically. "You either believe all of his promises or none of them. God doesn't make mistakes. Disabilities are not mistakes. God doesn't waste anything. Not one life."

After my birth, mom continued to visit the family-planning clinic in Salamá. She and Dad understood that too many children, born into a family without the means to care for them, would not be good stewardship of their bodies, their resources, and the lives that God had given under their care. They also knew that even the most carefully arranged human plans can be frustrated by God and that God's plans are higher and should be honored.

I am thankful that, in spite of the surprise that overturned science and planning, Mom and Dad decided to have me. It was my mom's choice, and she chose life.

Abortion and the Sanctity of Life

The issue of induced abortion has been one of the most divisive topics in modern societies since the establishment of family planning and modern obstetrics. In fact, there is documented evidence that American foreign-policy strategies have directly targeted abortion and family-planning efforts in some countries in order to effect population control or the reduction of maternal death due to unwanted or high-risk pregnancies.[1] The policies have exacerbated the cultural realities of male domination in many developing countries, where women have been primarily considered homemakers and child-bearers, giving preference to the birthing of boys in order to continue patriarchal traditions.

Due to policy and media pressures, particularly in the poor nations, the practices of family planning and induced abortions have clashed with local traditions. However, due to the pressures of foreign policies upon poor nations, governmental institutions carried them in those countries without any understanding of the cultural, ethical, and moral realities of the people. As a result, abortion has become rampant and uncontrolled in some places, creating major social and ethical problems for a large number of communities in the world. As the issue has become more prevalent around the world, the ethical and moral codes of poor societies have begun to shift to make room for foreign-aid policies that promote abortion and family planning as requirements for receiving aid.

For many years, and because of the pressures of foreign policies, abortion in poor nations has become as prevalent as it has been in industrialized nations. A recent study on the global incidence of abortion in the world reveals that, between 1990 and 2014, the number of abortions worldwide increased from 50.4 million in the period

---

1. Congressional Research Service, "Abortion and Family Planning-Related Provisions in U.S. Foreign Assistance Law and Policy," August 21, 2020, https://fas.org/sgp/crs/row/R41360.pdf.

between 1990 and 1994, to 56.3 million in the period between 2010 and 2014. The same study estimated that, in the last period under study (2010–2014), there were 35 abortions per 1,000 women aged 15–44 years worldwide. While the argument of the researchers was that the percentage of abortions per 1,000 child-bearing-age women had declined from the percentages of the first five years under analysis, the fact remains that more than 10 million induced abortions have been taking place every year around the world. Sadly, the same study determined that, in the same period, globally, 25 percent of pregnancies ended in abortion, with the larger share occurring in the developed world.[2]

Those who have argued on both sides of the abortion issue have used medical, human rights, and economic reasons to debate the legitimacy of terminating a pregnancy, and they have pitted the rights of the mother against the rights of the child in the central discussions. However, the question of abortion is not one of individual rights, or even of socioeconomic risk. The discussion should address the deeper ethical and moral question of the life that begins at conception and the personhood of a fetus.[3] Even the various expressions of the church worldwide have entered into the debate from the perspectives of economic considerations and the question of human rights rather than from the biblical perspective that affirms the beginning of life at the point of conception. As a result, induced abortion is more prevalent in developed countries dominated by Christianity, which in itself seems to be a theological and sociological paradox. Sadly, while the argument continues, millions of lives are ended every year.

---

2. G. Sedgh, et al., "Abortion incidence between 1990 and 2014: Global, regional, and subregional levels and trends" *Lancet* (July 16, 2016), 258–67.

3. Caitlin Borgmann, "The Meaning of Life: Belief and Reason in the Abortion Debate" (2009), *CUNY Academic Works*, http://academicworks.cuny.edu /cl_pubs/143.

In the case of developing nations, induced abortion takes place as a mixture of local tradition and foreign policies that target family planning. For example, in cultures with local religious practices that deem the birth of a girl to be a curse, parents resort to abortion to commit fetal femicide. Further, in many agrarian societies—where boys are favored over girls—traditional methods of induced abortion are used to prevent the births of unwanted girls. Ironically, those Western family-planning methods that argue against life at conception are the same ones that promote medical procedures to determine fetal gender so that "safer" abortions may take place.

It is in this context that I was born. In my mother's case, as may be true for thousands of women in the world, the issue couldn't be settled by affirming local tradition or embracing foreign policy. It may sound overly simplistic, but the issue of abortion would be easily settled if we truly understood and believed that life starts at conception, just as Scripture affirms. This truth was the compass that helped my mom make the decision not to terminate her high-risk pregnancy. Keeping me was her decision. It was her choice, formed and *in*formed by a strong ethical and moral code that she learned from Scripture.

What Does the Bible Say?

There is scriptural evidence to affirm that life starts at conception and that the person and character of each individual are genetically formed before birth. When God calls the prophet Jeremiah to fulfill the mission that God has for him, God reminds the prophet that God, in his sovereignty, set him apart even before his birth: "Before I formed you in the womb I knew you, before you were born I set you apart; I appointed you as a prophet to the nations" (Jeremiah 1:5). God was at work in Jeremiah's life long before he was born.

David also recognizes this divine reality when he thanks God for the wonderful formation of his personhood, his character, and his physical being, even while he was in his mother's womb: "For you created my inmost being; you knit me together in my mother's womb. I praise you because I am fearfully and wonderfully made; your works are wonderful, I know that full well. My frame was not hidden from you when I was made in the secret place, when I was woven together in the depths of the earth. Your eyes saw my unformed body; all the days ordained for me were written in your book before one of them came to be" (Psalm 139:13–16).

While these scriptural truths are definite evidence of God's design for life to begin at conception, there are those who wrongly argue that those statements are mere metaphors that conflict with science and genetics. To affirm the biblical truth and argument that our lives are defined from the time of conception and should not be terminated, experts on human embryology have made the following statement: "Life is a continuous process. Fertilization is a critical landmark because, under ordinary circumstances, a new, genetically distinct human organism is hereby formed. . . . The combination of 23 chromosomes present in each pronucleus results in 46 chromosomes in the zygote. Thus, the diploid number is restored and the embryonic genome is formed. The embryo now exists as a genetic unit."[4]

My mother may not have had a depth of scientific information to make her decision, but she knew from the teachings of the church and from her personal relationship with Christ that human life is sacred and that a new baby is a gift from God. Thanks to the prompting of the Holy Spirit and the teachings of the church, thousands of women like my mom can choose life as a gift.

Based on both Scripture and science, the spiritual family that I have the privilege to serve has taken a clear stand to preserve and protect the sanctity of life. This perspective, which is rooted in a

---

4. Ronan R. O'Rahili and Fabiola Müller, *Human Embryology & Teratology*, 2nd ed. (New York: Wiley-Liss, 1996), 8, 29.

Wesleyan tradition of social ethics, helps frame the question of abortion. We affirm:

> the sanctity of human life as established by God the Creator and believe that such sanctity extends to the child not yet born. Life is a gift from God. All human life, including life developing in the womb, is created by God in his image and is, therefore, to be nurtured, supported, and protected. From the moment of conception, a child is a human being with all of the developing characteristics of human life, and this life is dependent on the mother for its continued development. Therefore, we believe that human life must be respected and protected from the moment of conception. We oppose induced abortion by any means, when used for either personal convenience or population control. We oppose laws that allow abortion. Realizing that there are rare, but real medical conditions wherein the mother of the unborn child, or both, could not survive the pregnancy, termination of the pregnancy should only be made after sound medical and Christian counseling.

> Responsible opposition to abortion requires our commitment to the initiation and support of programs designed to provide care for mothers and children. The crisis of an unwanted pregnancy calls for the community of believers (represented only by those for whom knowledge of the crisis is appropriate) to provide a context of love, prayer, and counsel. In such instances, support can take the form of counseling centers, homes for expectant mothers, and the creation or utilization of Christian adoption services.

> [We] recognize that consideration of abortion as a means of ending an unwanted pregnancy often occurs because Christian standards of sexual responsibility have been ignored. Therefore the church calls for persons to practice the ethic of the New Testament as it bears upon human sexuality and to deal with the issue

of abortion by placing it within the larger framework of biblical principles that provide guidance for moral decision making.

[We] also recognize that many have been affected by the tragedy of abortion. Each local congregation and individual believer is urged to offer the message of forgiveness by God for each person who has experienced abortion. Our local congregations are to be communities of redemption and hope to all who suffer physical, emotional, and spiritual pain as a result of the willful termination of a pregnancy.[5]

---

5. Church of the Nazarene, *Manual: 2017–2021* (Kansas City, MO: Nazarene Publishing House, 2017), 51–52.

2
ALMOST
LEFT FOR DEAD

UNFORTUNATELY, the doctor who predicted dire consequences should my mother go ahead with her pregnancy was not completely off base. Weeks after my birth, Mom realized there was something wrong with my health. I wasn't able to retain any of the nutrients that she gave me when she fed me. She tried all kinds of home remedies and alternative foods that she could find in our small town but to no avail. Weeks went by, and I was not gaining any weight. On the contrary, in fact, I was showing signs of early malnutrition and dehydration caused by gastrointestinal diseases—evidenced by, among other things, constant vomiting and diarrhea. It was a bleak picture, and the clinic in town didn't have an answer, so my mother again decided to take the long, dusty, two-hour trip by bus to Salamá and see the doctor.

It was the same doctor who saw her during her pregnancy, which is not uncommon in rural hospitals in developing countries. These hospitals often have one doctor, a couple of nurses, a small operating room, a few inpatient beds, and basic medications in the pharmacy (if any medicine at all). Mom waited for hours to get a number for the doctor to see her. Sometimes patients are fortunate to get a number that allows them to be seen on the same day, but that is a rare occurrence. Many times, patients stay with relatives, in guesthouses, and even on open patios for nights at a time in hopes of being seen soon by the doctor. As a side note, it appears that Mom became an expert on those visits because this was only the first of many more to come.

"I told you so!" were the first words the doctor uttered when my mom relayed my symptoms. "I am not surprised at all—he was not supposed to live. You brought him into this world to suffer, and you are now suffering with him," he added. Mom silently endured the physician's scolding. He was the doctor, after all, and she wanted him to see and diagnose me. She hoped to hear something positive about treatment. Unfortunately, this was not the case.

"Your child is basically going to die in the next couple of hours. He is dehydrated, and his gastric system isn't developed enough to hold any food—not now, not ever. Leave him in the room next door and go home," he ordered.

"The room next door" turned out to be a dark room where dozens of children under five years of age were left to die because they were suffering from diseases that, though preventable, had put them at risk of death, and they were left to become numbers in the infant-mortality statistics of villages in the developing world. Later in life I discovered that many peasant families do not even name or register their children until after they have made it past their first year because they don't want to waste a name or the money required to register a child if the child isn't even going to live. Mom told me that she took a peek into the room next door. All she could see and smell was death. Children in that room didn't even have the energy to cry. They were left there to die because their parents could not afford—whether with time, money, or energy—to care for them.

I cannot imagine what went through the mind of my young mother as she stood at the door of "the room next door," burdened already with the knowledge of her seven healthy children and husband back home, all of whom needed and required her time and attention. What if the doctor had been right from the very beginning? What if I was not going to make it after all and she was just stubbornly and unwisely sacrificing herself and the rest of our family? I don't know what other mothers would have done. It was evident that many of them had already followed the doctor's recommendation and left their young children in that room to die. But my mother ignored the doctor once again.

The trip back to San Jerónimo must have felt like eternity for her. She was leaving Salamá with no answers and no knowledge about how to care for me. All she knew was that she was defying doctor's orders once again. I was supposed to be left for dead, and she was supposed to go back home—empty-handed, grieving, and exhausted.

Exhausted she was. She took the bus home, riding for two long hours through the ten-mile section of rock and dust that separated the hospital with its "room next door" from our home, where her family waited. Our house was not much, but even if I was going to die, my mom decided that at least I deserved a Christian death, with a Christian funeral, with my Christian family surrounding me, in my Christian home. I was not going to be left for dead. I had a name, after all! Ironically, I had been named after my mom's uncle, who had died while she was pregnant with me from electrocution by lightning.

The bus arrived in San Jerónimo. Since it was such a small town with only one street that cut across it during its entire half-mile length, the bus only made two stops—one at the entrance to the town and one at the exit. Our home, which shared real estate with the telegraph and post office, was located in the *barrio arriba* (or, "uptown"), closer to the park and the end of the road. So Mom stayed on the bus with the dying baby until it stopped and everyone else had gotten off.

Those who planted the first evangelical church in San Jerónimo had been known for being missionary folks. Ever since their establishment, Holiness missionaries have planted churches in strategic locations in towns, villages, and cities, and San Jerónimo was no exception. In the case of my hometown, missionaries planted a Nazarene church at the end of the road with the hope and vision that the place would be a strategic hub in the years to come. When they built the church there was no bus service between San Jerónimo and Salamá. The only transportation was a bus that traveled from the country's capital, Ciudad de Guatemala (Guatemala City), to the department's capital, Salamá, by way of San Jerónimo twice a week. That bus stopped in front of the church, and it became the natural terminal for the new service that, years later, connected the two towns through the dusty, ten-mile stretch.

That's where Mom got off the bus—in front of the church where, seven years earlier, my dad had given his heart to Christ and where she, a year after seeing my dad's transformation, left her religious tradition and joined the church to live a life of love, service, and holiness.

Fortunately, these were the years that the church was open 24/7. Mom got off the bus and walked across the street. It was late afternoon on a weekday, and the church was empty. She entered the sanctuary with a dying baby in her arms. The doctor had decided the baby's future. All that was left was to let her son die peacefully at home. But Mom told me that she walked down the aisle—the same aisle she had walked years earlier when she and Dad decided to get married after years of living together and already having had four children. She walked down the aisle with tears in her eyes but with the certainty that "God doesn't do crooked things, and even sad things work for good for those who love him."

She put me on the altar and prayed, "God, you have created this child. He is yours. I give him to you for your glory, for your honor, and to your will." She waited and prayed until she felt at peace. "May your will be done," she said, and left the church to go home.

On her way home, she met Doña Maria, the midwife who had delivered me, as well as some of my older siblings. Doña Maria was a simple woman with no formal education. She was a peasant who had been trained by her ancestors in the art and science of midwifery. She had delivered most of the babies in town and in the surrounding villages, and she was known for her wisdom and humble counsel.

"What's with you, Doña Emma?" she said to my mom. "You look tired, and it seems that you have been crying a lot."

Mom told her what the doctor had said, and shared that she was on her way home to await the will of God.

Doña Maria offered a quick diagnosis: "His problem is that he doesn't have enough worms! Give the boy a soup that will create worms and defenses in his body. Go to the market, buy a pound of beef tripe, and boil. Add some water; then give him the broth. Less than a cup will do it. By tomorrow, he will have such a fever that you will think he is burning. After the fever, he will either die or survive. Two days is all it takes. Hurry!"

Mom went to the meat market and knocked. It was late, but she didn't have time to waste. With a high dose of faith, a grain of hope, and a bit of courage, she made the soup, gave me some of it, and went to bed. The following day was a hard one. The family waited in prayer. As Doña Maria had predicted, I burned with a fever that lasted for hours. I convulsed, and my eyes turned completely white. It looked like death would win.

When morning came, however, the fever was gone. Two more days went by, and—just as the midwife had said—Mom's faith and resilience had paid off. I survived the odds that were stacked against me. Thirty years later, my mother told me this story when I asked her what she had meant by what she'd said to Louie Bustle in that dining room Ecuador. She said, "You were weeks old when I gave you to the Lord. It has been the Lord's business ever since."

Decades later, when I had children of my own, mom always insisted on celebrating first birthdays "with pomp and circumstance." She told me that, having seen so many children die before they celebrated their first birthdays, she made it a practice to celebrate big whenever their children survived their first year. "Reaching one year of age in our countries is a miracle and a gift to celebrate," she often said.

Infant Mortality and Child Survival

Sadly, my case was not rare in our country. The fact that the small, rural hospital had a "room next door" for children to be left to die was not unique to Salamá or Guatemala. Infant mortality was a rampant problem in the 1960s, and it still is in most of the developing world.

Early in 2020, the world was affected by the news of a global pandemic that ended up impacting the health, mobility, and economy of the entire world. By the end of July 2020, the COVID-19 virus had taken the lives of more than 675,000 people worldwide.[1] This number represents a rough estimate of more than 3,000 deaths per day during the height of the first wave. These numbers are staggering, and they are a reflection of a global disease that brought the world to a halt and created havoc in the lives of communities, congregations, and countries.

As dramatic as the numbers were for this pandemic that captured the attention of the global news media, the last century in modernity has missed the staggering numbers of child mortality—a daily, worldwide tragedy that has rarely made headlines. In 2017, which was believed to be representative of one of the best decades

---

1. World Health Organization (WHO): "Coronavirus disease (COVID-19) Situation Report—194," August 1, 2020, https://www.who.int/docs/default-source /coronaviruse/situation-reports/20200801-covid-19-sitrep-194.pdf?s fvrsn=401287f3_2.

in modern history for child-survival numbers, 5.4 million children died before they reached their fifth birthday. This means that, on an average day, 15,000 children under the age of five died, mainly of preventable disease.[2]

One of the reasons for the world to ignore or dismiss the numbers of child deaths is that the problem has become historically endemic. Even developed societies in their recent modern history have records of families losing between two or three children at a time when fertility rates and child mortality rates were equally high. As the world developed, countries made inroads in the fight against infant mortality. Nevertheless, in poor nations, the average family is not exonerated from counting at least one child lost to malnutrition, gastrointestinal diseases, malaria, or other preventable illnesses. Currently, a high percentage of these deaths occur in the poorest nations of the world, where an estimated five million deaths (or roughly 93 percent) are children under the age of five. In fact, one of the key development indicators in the world is the infant mortality rate. There is evidence that nations with higher development indicators show low infant mortality rates.[3]

Sadly, a large percentage of those deaths can be attributed to the consequences of poverty and social neglect. A 1995 study on the causes of child mortality in the world revealed that an estimated 70 percent of the deaths of children under five years of age were attributed to malaria, acute respiratory infections, diarrheal illness, malnutrition, and immunizable diseases.[4] In other words, a vast majority

2. Max Roser, Hannah Ritchie, and Bernadeta Dadonaite, "Child and Infant Mortality," *Our World in Data* (published 2013; updated November 2019), https://ourworldindata.org/child-mortality.

3. Tim Dyson, "Infant and Child Mortality in Developing Countries," in R. K. Chandra (ed.), *Critical Reviews in Tropical Medicine*, vol. 2 (New York: Plenum Press, 1984), 39–76.

4. D. L. Pelletier, E. A. Frongillo, Jr, D. G. Schroeder, and J. P. Habicht, "The Effects of Malnutrition on Child Mortality in Developing Countries" *Bulle-*

of infant deaths were caused by situations and diseases that could have been easily prevented through access to preventive healthcare, sanitation, and nutrition.

This was the environment in which I was born. In 1963, the infant mortality rate in Guatemala was 140.5.[5] This means that, for every 1,000 children who were born that year, more than 140 died before they reached the age of 5. Considering that our small town was rated among the poorest, unhealthiest towns in the country, all eight of my parents' children reaching age five was considered an exception and not the norm. My mother came from a large family, and she lost several infant siblings. My death would have been just another statistic, but by God's grace and my mother's resilience, it wasn't.

What Does the Bible Say?

Child mortality due to poverty and social evil has never been part of God's plan. God's plan for creation is that all live the abundant life God has prepared for us. Children are expected to grow and flourish as modeled in Scripture. Both Samuel and Jesus, as children, are described as growing in "wisdom" and "stature" and "in favor" with both God and other people (see 1 Samuel 2:26; Luke 2:52).

As the Bible reveals it, God designed us to grow holistically from the very first moment in our lives. Growing in wisdom, stature, and favor with God and people means holistic child development from the time of conception—when our organs, our genetic personality, and our identity are being developed—to the time that we grow into responsible adults. This means that, from the very beginning, children are designed to experience mental and cognitive growth (wisdom), physical growth (stature), social growth (favor with people), and spiritual growth (favor with God). The concept of the whole per-

---

tin of the World Health Organization (1995), 73 (4), pp. 443–448.

5. Macrotrends, "Guatemala Infant Mortality Rate 1950–2021," https://www.macrotrends.net/countries/GTM/Guatemala/infant-mortality-rate.

son is not something that happens once we are adults. On the contrary, as Scripture clearly states, Christ and the prophets model for us how children are to grow.

Children growing into responsible and healthy adulthood is one of the symbols of God's restoration of all things. In Isaiah's description of new creation—the new Jerusalem—God promises that "never again will there be in [the new Jerusalem] an infant who lives but a few days" (Isaiah 65:20a). This promise emphasizes that the premature death of children should not be considered normal, especially when the causes are easily preventable social and physical illnesses.

Growing up in the church, I became aware of that promise. We are taught that children are special in the kingdom of God and that the kingdom of heaven belongs to them, and I have made sure in my adult ministry that this truth is ingrained in the minds of church members. In fact, most of the early years of my ministry were intentionally focused on the holistic development of children in their communities. The fact that children are precious in God's eyes has been a driving force in most of my ministry and mission life. I saw that emphasis and passion rewarded in 2009 when my denomination became the first global evangelical body to state clearly in their polity around social issues the value of children and youth:

The Bible commands every Christian to "speak up for those who cannot speak for themselves, for the rights of all who are destitute" (Proverbs 31:8). The Shema (Deuteronomy 6:4–7; 11:19) admonishes us to communicate God's grace to our children. Psalm 78:4 declares, "We will tell the next generation the praiseworthy deeds of the LORD, his power, and the wonders he has done." Jesus affirms this in Luke 18:16, "Let the little children come to me, and do not hinder them, for the kingdom of God belongs to such as these."

As a response to this biblical perspective, [we] acknowledge that children are important to God and a priority in his kingdom. We believe God directed us to attend to all children—to love, nurture, protect, uphold, guide, and advocate for them. It is God's plan that we introduce children to the life of salvation and growth in grace. Salvation, holiness, and discipleship are possible and imperative in the lives of children. We recognize that children are not a means to an end, but full participants in the body of Christ. Children are disciples in training, not disciples in waiting.

Thus, holistic and transformational ministry to children and their families in every local church will be a priority as evidenced by:

- providing effective and empowering ministries to the whole child—physically, mentally, emotionally, socially, and spiritually;
- articulating Christian positions on current social justice issues that affect children;
- connecting children to the heart of the mission and ministry of the faith community;
- discipling children and training them to disciple others;
- equipping parents to nurture the spiritual formation of their children.

. . . [We] envision an intergenerational faith community where children and youth are loved and valued, where they are ministered to and incorporated into the church family through a wide variety of means and methods, and where they have opportunities to minister to others in ways consistent with their ages, development, abilities, and spiritual gifts.[6]

If children matter to God, then they must also matter to us.

---

6. Church of the Nazarene, *Manual: 2017–2021*, 398–99.

3
ALMOST
BLIND

BEFORE I WAS THREE MONTHS OLD, I had to face yet another challenge: the genetic gift of partial blindness due to strabismus in the left eye. While this was not completely evident during the first weeks of my life, we found out that the eye problem was exacerbated by the convulsions and high fevers that were caused by my gastric problems. Although I was born with partial sight, my eyes soon turned completely white, and my pupils turned toward the inside in what the doctors called "an acute case of strabismus in both eyes." I became practically blind. My siblings tell me that the only way I could see my hands was by literally turning my head and following my hands until the pupil of one of my eyes made the connection with them.

With eight poor children and the youngest practically blind, my mother decided to skip medical care in Salamá and instead try Guatemala City. She had two siblings living there, and they told her there was a brand-new charity in the country that had been established to help the blind and deaf. The Guatemalan Foundation for the Blind and Deaf had just started a campaign in Guatemala with the purpose of eradicating diseases that are generally connected to poor nutrition and healthcare. I remember Mom telling me that we would first travel to the city, leaving the family behind in San Jerónimo for at least two weeks in order to go every morning to the eye clinic to try to get a number to be seen by the doctor. Mom and I would stay at her sister's home and wait until an appointment became available, and only then begin to hope for the doctor to be available and willing to take my case.

By God's grace, after several expensive trips to the city, Mom finally got an appointment with the eye doctor. The doctor ordered intensive eye-corrective therapy at home, and my mother—busy though she was, caring for a large family and plying her trade as a seamstress—faithfully kept up the daily therapy with the hope that at least one of my eyes would be corrected. The therapy worked relatively well, and within a couple of months, my right eye started to show signs of progress.

I had my first pair of glasses when I was nine months old—a true miracle. In our case, the only way to address the partial blindness and hopefully avoid the complete loss of my eyesight was to get public assistance from a distant charity in Guatemala City. To be seen by one of the pioneer eye doctors in the country required persistence and, as people back home used to say, "a bit of good fortune." (It actually required God's miraculous intervention to connect all the dots.) It took months of plain faith and therapy to help one of my eyes self-correct, and then it was time to enter the ten-year journey toward full recovery of my eyesight.

My elementary-school years were marked by being the only child in school who wore glasses and had a left eye completely crossed. It was not unusual for children at school to mock me because of my frail constitution, my large glasses, and my left crossed eye. However, I don't recall feeling sad, offended, or ashamed because of my condition. Somehow, the Lord had equipped me to cope with an intense desire to live, to survive, and to thrive. The visits to the city to see the eye doctor (and other doctors who treated the many health conditions of a poor, sickly child) became the norm. Glasses became part of me, and there were times when I woke up without my glasses on and started crying because I wasn't used to being awake without them.

In 1973, the eye doctor who saw me at the charity's hospital decided to pioneer a surgical treatment to repair crossed eyes in children. He told my mother I was a good candidate for the procedure and, in November of 1974, when I was eleven and had just finished elementary school, I became one of the first cases of corrective pediatric eye surgery performed at the foundation's hospital. It was perhaps one of the most traumatic experiences of my life.

Surgery was relatively successful. I woke up from the anesthesia after three hours in the operating room to find both my eyes covered. My mother had been told they were going to operate only on the left eye, but because the damage to my eye muscles had been severe, the doctors ended up operating in both eyes to correct the condition. I was left with bandages on both eyes for a minimum of three very long days. In spite of my limitations, I had still managed to see out of one eye for the first ten years of my life, so it was unnerving to find myself in the solitude of a cold hospital with silence around me and both eyes covered. My mother told me that I was so desperate to remove the bandages that the doctors threatened to tie my hands to the bed to keep me from impeding my recovery.

I came out of the hospital with both eyes straightened. I couldn't see myself in the mirror for at least a couple of weeks because both eyes were completely bloodshot. The recovery process was slow, and from time to time I wondered if I *would* recover. I didn't know what the future held for me, but by year's end, I was able to wear sunglasses and prepare for middle school in a new setting, with people who didn't know I had been cross-eyed for more than a decade.

Unfortunately, the damage to the optic nerve in my left eye was irreversible. The corrective surgery was successful in the sense that I no longer had a visibly crossed eye, but I never fully recovered the vision in that eye, despite therapy and vision exercises, and I was officially diagnosed as partially blind in the left eye. Nevertheless, I was thankful because the doctor had corrected the orientation of my eyes, and I was already used to seeing with only one eye.

The condition of partial blindness was never an issue for me until my last years in architecture school in Guatemala. When I was nearing the completion of my education, we were required to take a class on land survey. Since it was the early 1980s, the concept of stereoscopy was new in the academic world. We were using stereoscopic glasses to determine the depth and height of land and buildings through the juxtaposition of aerial photos. All my classmates were fascinated by the technology, but I wasn't. I thought my stereoscope was damaged, and I asked the instructor to replace it, but the results were the same. I couldn't for the life of me see things in three dimensions through the use of 3D lenses.

After much frustration, the instructor asked me if I had any eye problems that might prevent me from seeing things in 3D.

"I am blind in my left eye," I told him.

His amused reply came back, "We need both eyes to have a good sense of depth perception!"

Up to that day, for more than twenty years, I had never known the difference. My right eye had thus far been sufficient to see and enjoy the world around me and to contemplate the beauty of God's creation through the gift of eyesight.

Blindness and Eye Care for the Poor and Vulnerable

In the early 2000s, it is estimated that nearly nineteen million children worldwide suffered from serious vision problems that would affect their normal development, hurting them psychologically, socially, educationally, and economically. Furthermore, it is estimated that nearly 90 percent of the children who face visual impairment in the world are impoverished, which makes it difficult for them to access the basic healthcare needed to improve their vision. Unfortunately, unlike other global diseases affecting the world, blindness among children has only increased with the passage of time.[1]

As if poverty and blindness were not enough of a burden for poor children and their families, visual impairment places them into an aggravated cycle of poverty, which results in many of these disadvantaged children ending up on the streets, begging, and even being trafficked due to their disabilities. Children with vision loss struggle to learn in school, which puts them behind in the economic chain. As they grow older, they find it difficult to get a job, which sinks them further into poverty. As with many disabled children in poor countries, visually impaired children carry the burden of the social tag that already places them at a disadvantage with the rest of the world.

The insidious combination of poverty and blindness has proven to be tragic, even lethal, particularly in those countries deprived of social welfare mechanisms. Social science studies performed in extremely poor countries in the world point out that 50 to 60 percent of children die within one to two years of becoming blind, not only because of the associated diseases that created the blindness but also because of neglect.[2]

---

1. Kovin Naidoo and Courtenay Holden, "Why So Many Children around the World Could Go Blind," Our Children's Vision, https://ourchildrensvision .org/blog/item/53-why-so-many-children-around-the-world-could-go-blind .html.

2. Brien A. Holden, "Blindness and Poverty: A Tragic Combination," *Clinical and Experimental Optometry* (2007), 90:6, 401–03.

When one considers the risk that a disabled child represents to the economy of a poor family, one might understand the medical advice the doctor gave my mother when she was pregnant in spite of contraception. His view that a disabled child would add extra burden to the already taxed family economy made sense. Yet my mother decided that it was up to God and that she was not going to get in God's way.

What Does the Bible Say?

In his study of the theology of blindness in the Hebrew Scriptures, Ray McAllister observes that, in Scripture, "blindness is described as a most devastating condition, especially when compared with other physical disabilities."[3] Through a survey of the entire Old Testament, he concludes that blindness was interpreted by religious leaders as an abnormality that was either caused by the blind person's sin or as a penalty to sinful parents on a newborn child. McAllister also concluded that, while these were the religious interpretations of the time, the biblical principles affirmed that the blind were not to be rejected or discriminated against because "the blind are loved by God, and so must be treated with compassion and dignity, and allowed to function as freely as physically possible while recognizing their limitations."[4]

This reality is emphasized by Jesus's ministry to the blind. When he started his ministry and made his declaration of mission in what is known as "the Nazareth Manifesto" in Luke 4, Jesus quoted the prophecy of Isaiah 61:1–2: "The Spirit of the Lord is on me, because he has anointed me to proclaim good news to the poor. He has sent me to proclaim freedom for the prisoners and recovery of

---

3. Ray McAllister, "Theology of Blindness in the Hebrew Scriptures," *Dissertations*, 89 (Andrews University, 2010), https://digitalcommons.andrews.edu/dissertations/89.

4. McAllister, "Theology of Blindness," 368.

sight for the blind, to set the oppressed free, to proclaim the year of the Lord's favor" (Luke 4:18–19). Because of the binding nature of blindness, Jesus made sure people understood that his ministry was for those who were marginalized by any condition that would place them short of the image of God designed for them.

John 9 introduces us to a story that reflects the cultural and religious interpretations of blindness in the context of faith and society during Jesus's time. The disciples were arguing over whether a man blind from birth was blind because of his own sin or that of his parents. The disciples were affected by the theological and sociological biases that had already determined that blindness was a punishment for sin. For the disciples, marginality and rejection were normal for this person who had been born with a physical limitation that they deemed a punishment.

Not so for Jesus. Rather than entering a socio-theological debate about the sinful reality of blindness, Jesus took the opportunity to seize the moment and allow the work of God to be displayed in this man's life. Jesus's compassionate and inclusive response to the theological and sociological patterns of the world were to highlight that there is no physical limitation that can prevent us from seeing the mighty work of God through the people of God in the hands of Jesus.

To the shock of the blind man's neighbors and family, those who were accustomed to his status of marginality and disability, Jesus restored more than the man's sight. He restored his dignity. He allowed him to be reinserted into society as an equal to everybody else. At the end of the chapter, the blind man encountered the fullness of sight when he met Jesus and worshiped him as his Lord and Savior.

For years my mother took me to the center for the blind and deaf for my annual checkups. She never saw me as a liability or as a disabled child. She saw me as a child created in God's image, and she believed that God had the power to restore my sight entirely and the sovereignty to allow me to live with my visual limitations. Intuitively, and thanks to the teaching of the church, my parents believed in the power of divine healing. This is what the church taught them: "We believe in the biblical doctrine of divine healing and urge our people to offer the prayer of faith for the healing of the sick. We also believe God heals through the means of medical science."[5]

I praise God for his healing touch upon my eyes. I am thankful for my mother's patience in giving me daily therapy in spite of her busy schedule caring for a large, poor family. And I am thankful for the miracles of science and technology, which God used to provide healing and sight for me and still uses to do the same for many other children in similar circumstances.

5. Church of the Nazarene, "XIV: Divine Healing," *Manual: 2017–2021*, 35.

4
ALMOST NOMADIC

SAN JERÓNIMO is a beautiful Guatemalan town. Nested in the center of a green and productive valley, this charming town that the Dominican missionaries chose to make the center of their production of sugarcane and wine during colonial times was, however, forgotten by years of underdevelopment and governmental abuse. By the time my family was established in San Jerónimo in the late 1960s, the majority of the population worked in agriculture, and children's only access to education was the local elementary school. There was no middle or secondary school, so the only way for parents to continue their children's education beyond grade school was to send them away to boarding schools.

My family was no exception. Mom and Dad always believed that education was the most fundamental resource that would help people break the cycle of poverty. When my oldest sister, Vilma, was ready to go to secondary school, she was sent to a government dorm in Chiquimula, a town located days away from our home. Then came my second and third siblings, and my parents also sent them away to study while living in private dorms. Education was becoming unaffordable, but they were committed to educating their children. Mom increased her hours working as a seamstress to help supplement Dad's income as a civil servant so their children could improve their odds of working in professions that could help them earn a living.

When the time came for Anny, the fourth child, to go to secondary school, my parents could no longer afford the expense of room and board, so they decided not to send her to school. When our maternal grandparents found out she was not going to study, they agreed to let her live with them on the condition that she would work in their home, helping with domestic chores, while studying in night school. Since there was no other option, my parents sent Anny away with the hope that things would work out.

Unfortunately, things didn't work out. With four of her children scattered across the country, Mom felt as if her family were splintered, and she wasn't even sure it was for the best. Nobody was guaranteed a better life. Mom convinced Dad to move out of San Jerónimo to pursue work so the rest of the children could have more opportunities to access education and a better life. Months later, Dad was transferred to Cobán, where he continued working as a telegrapher, and the entire family moved there. While my oldest three siblings continued their studies outside the home, Anny left our grandparents' house to return to live with the family in Cobán. The year was 1969.

Cobán is a picturesque town located in the heart of the northern mountains of Guatemala. Because of its weather, legend has it that

King Charles V decided to make Cobán one of his summer locations while running the Spanish empire. The locals still recall this historical choice and have nicknamed Cobán "the Imperial City." Cobán also has a special place in the heart of Holiness missions. In 1904 the first missionaries arrived to pioneer the work of the Holiness Movement. The arrival of the missionaries was congruent with the strategy of evangelization for Guatemala, which divided the nation among five large evangelical denominations from the United States and England in order to evangelize the nation and maintain a harmonious missionary work. Holiness groups were assigned to the north of the country, which resulted in the rapid growth and expansion of churches in places like Las Verapaces—the two regions to the north of Guatemala City.

As committed and thankful believers from San Jerónimo, my parents joined the Church of the Nazarene in Cobán and participated with them in the history of one of the most vibrant districts in the Nazarene family worldwide. Central Church of the Nazarene in Cobán, which my parents joined in 1969, was the first Holiness church in the country, and it has given birth to hundreds of new congregations, raised hundreds of leaders, and sponsored more than ten districts. Thanks to the connectedness of the Nazarene family, my parents—migrants from Baja Verapaz—were soon welcomed in the church, and the family quickly found a home. My parents joined Central Church of the Nazarene in Cobán in the year that the church celebrated its golden jubilee—Central was the first Nazarene church organized in Guatemala on August 11, 1919.[1]

Because of weather, health, and other reasons that a six-year-old would not fully know or understand, the family decided to move again in what sociologists often refer to as "step migration." They moved

---

1. Providentially, I had the privilege to be the preacher at the centennial celebration for Central Church of the Nazarene in Cobán on August 10–11, 2019—fifty years after my family joined in 1969.

from a small town to a regional capital and then to the nation's capital. The plan was to give the entire family access to education, job opportunities, and the possibility of breaking the cycle of poverty that had entrapped my family for many years. By March of 1970, the entire family had moved to Mixco, one of the municipalities surrounding the metropolitan area of Guatemala City. Since two of my siblings were still attending school in various other cities and one of them had dropped out of school to get married, the family unit that moved to the city comprised Mom, Dad, and five children. This group of seven, who had lived in a rather large home (albeit with dusty floors, no running water, and limited electricity), now lived in the crowded confinement of one room in a house shared by at least three other families. There we were, intimidated by the big city and overcrowded in one small room but united and hopeful about the educational and economic opportunities that the city would present to us.

My stay in Mixco didn't last long. By the end of 1969, my sister Vilma, the oldest, had graduated as a schoolteacher at the age of twenty, and she had to look for a job "anywhere in the country" in order to help the family with raising the rest of her siblings. In my sister's words, she had "reaped the benefits of education and access to work so that her siblings could now benefit from her blessings." In what was really a miracle, and only months after her graduation, she was hired for a job as a teacher of a one-room school in a remote village up in the mountains close to San Jerónimo, where we had previously lived—nearly one hundred miles away from where the family currently lived.

With my sister living by herself in a remote village in a rustic, wooden room attached to the classroom, my parents decided it was not safe for her to be alone, so they shipped me off to be her companion and student. At the age of six, almost seven, I was sent to live with my sister in Las Limas—a remote, very poor, and isolated village in a remote, very poor part of the country. I have few memories of that time, but I still recall the nights when the only lights we saw were from the candles we lit before going to bed or the occasional lights of a vehicle that would drive through the mountains once or twice during the night. My heart and mind still recall the sounds of the forest and the water lulling me to sleep while my sister said her daily prayers of thanksgiving and trust in the Lord. The year that we spent together in the middle of rural Guatemala allowed my sister and me to become strong siblings, and she became almost my second mother.

This was just the beginning of my nomadic life. I was told that my being nomadic comes from my great-grandparents from my dad's side. Dad used to tell me that his grandparents had traveled to Guatemala from Europe searching for a peaceful and quiet life on the new continent. I have tried to find with certainty the location from where they arrived, but the only thing I know is that they were also nomadic. I recently ventured to conduct genetic testing to determine the origins of my ancestors, just to find out that 54 percent of my DNA story can be traced to the Iberian Peninsula in Europe (Spain and Portugal), while 30 percent of my DNA has its roots in the indigenous peoples of Central America.

When I was seventeen and searching for new adventures after graduating from high school, I decided to study German with the eventual goal of migrating to Germany. I had grown fascinated by all things German. I had attended a German high school in the south of the country—where I went by myself at age fourteen—and I had just been hired to work for a German telecommunications company as one of their "whiz kids" in technology. I applied to a scholarship program to go to Germany to study engineering, and I was awarded it, but, much to my disappointment, it turned out that I was not old enough to go by myself. My dream to return to the continent of my dad's ancestors did not come true—at least not right away.

I did finally make it to Germany more than twenty years later, in 2004, when I was elected to a church leadership post whose regional office was located there. When I was a teenager, my nomadic dream to migrate to Germany to study engineering went unfulfilled, and

I eventually came to believe my study of the German language had been a waste of time. But in the end, the dream of a migrant to live in the land of his European great-grandparents *was* fulfilled—not on my terms but on God's terms.

Perhaps those early years traveling from village to town and back prepared me for later life as a missionary and itinerant servant. By the time I celebrated my fiftieth birthday, I had lived on four continents and I traveled doing God's missionary work to the last, the least, and the lost in more than one hundred countries across five continents. We have not stopped moving, yet I have deep in my heart a sense of home. There is a piece of Guatemala in my heart; the United States has become home for my family and me; and everywhere I go—like my parents when they moved to Cobán—I find family in the global church of God.

Global Migration, Internally Displaced People, and Refugees

Mobility is a human reality. Throughout history, humanity has witnessed and participated in waves of internal and external migration as part of its survival patterns. Thus, human migration has been a topic of extensive research and debate, and those who have studied human mobility and migration have concluded that the overwhelming causes of voluntary migration are economic. "When people are asked their reasons for moving, their better prospects in the urban economy usually stand out."[2] The quest for a land of promise and prosperity has motivated human exploration and migration in every century of our history. By 2020, there were an estimated 272 million international migrants, most of whom left their homes for work or in search of economic well-being.[3]

---

2. Alan Gilbert and Josef Gugler, *Cities, Poverty, and Development: Urbanization in the Third World* (New York: Oxford University Press, 1984), 52.

3. Charlotte Edmond, "Global Migration, By the Numbers: Who Migrates, Where They Go and Why," *World Economic Forum*, January 10, 2020, https://

For those searching for better economic prospects, migration normally happens through what has been known as step migration—that is, people moving from a rural area to the nearest town, searching for work. Step migration is incremental, allowing people to remain connected to the communities they have left, with the ability to return on a regular basis. As opportunities and personal and economic development in the nearest town change, people may continue to move from the nearest town to a larger economic hub. As conditions improve and more opportunities arise, people continue exploring forward and migrating until they transition from internal migration to international migration. This process is not new. The history of humanity has been shaped by the natural migration of people searching for better economic opportunities and a more prosperous livelihood for their families.

Unfortunately, not all human migration is catalyzed voluntarily by the search for economic prosperity. A significant number of people who migrate are forced to because their lives are at risk due to war, violence, and/or political instability. The political and social reality of millions of people today is that exile, displacement, and migration are not optional. By 2015, for example, the United Nations High Commissioner on refugees reported that there were nearly 58 million displaced people in the world, 15 million of whom were refugees or people in refugee-like situations.[4] Throughout human history, wars, internal conflicts, and occupations have been responsible for shaping the migration patterns of entire people groups. In fact, the history of many modern nations can be traced to a process of international migration caused by either persecution or wars.

---

www.weforum.org/agenda/2020/01/iom-global-migration-report-international-migrants-2020/.

4. Bo H. Lim, "Exile and Migration: Toward a Biblical Theology of Immigration and Displacement," *The Covenant Quarterly*, vol. 74 no. 2 (2016), 3.

For my immediate family, internal migration was precipitated by the search for educational opportunities because my parents firmly believed education was one of the keys to breaking the pernicious cycle of poverty. They left their families and even relative comfort to allow their children to access more education than they themselves had been able to have.

This has also been the reality for many of the nations where we currently live. The Americas were settled by indigenous people groups thousands of years before Christ came, yet what we know about our cultures and nations resulted from the exploration and exploitation of resources by the European settlers who arrived on this continent in the late 1490s, searching for new economic and political opportunities. All continents in the world are continents of immigrants—lands that have been populated either by people looking for a better, more prosperous future or by people escaping persecution, war, and famine.

What Does the Bible Say?

A significant portion of Scripture is developed around the narrative of immigration. A vast majority of biblical literature is structured under the reality of exploration, exodus, or exile, which gives us the proper perspective with regard to the immigrant, the foreigner, and the refugee:

- Abram left his country, his people, and his father's household to go to a land of a promise that God gave him (Genesis 12:1).
- Joseph was trafficked by his brothers and sent to the land of Egypt (Genesis 37:28). He was later used by God to help his family migrate from Canaan to Egypt during a massive famine (Genesis 46:3–7).
- God's people were slaves in Egypt for hundreds of years, so God called Moses to lead the people out of Egypt (Exodus 3:1–10).

- For forty years, God's people wandered in the wilderness, hoping to reach the promised land (Exodus 16:35; Numbers 32:13; Deuteronomy 2:7; 8:2; 29:5; Joshua 5:6).
- God's people were taken captive and into exile for seventy years (Jeremiah 29:10).
- The first-century church was established in various places around the ancient world because of, among other things, the persecution that pushed believers outside their lands (Acts 8:1).

Because of this history of mobility that God has allowed throughout history, God has always had a special provision for the immigrant, the refugee, and the foreigner. There are numerous scriptures that highlight God's heart for the landless. In both the Old Testament and the New Testament, God reminds his people that, since we all have, at one point in our lives, been transient, immigrants, or exiles, we must foster a special love, care, and dispensation for those who have been pushed out of their lands, their families, and their comforts to be among us.

In their November 2015 message to the global Wesleyan family, members of the Global Wesleyan Alliance echoed this sentiment of solidarity and love for the immigrant, the refugee, and the displaced person:

The Hebrew word *gēr* and the Greek word *xenos* can be defined as "immigrant."

"If an immigrant dwells with you in your land, you shall not mistreat him. The immigrant who dwells among you shall be to you as one born among you, and you shall love him as yourself" (Leviticus 19:33–34, NKJV). Our Lord quoted, "Love him as yourself" as part of the Greatest Commandment!

Jesus said: "I was hungry and you gave me something to eat, I was thirsty and you gave me something to drink, I was an immigrant and you invited me in" (Matthew 25:35, NIV).

"Do not forget to show hospitality to immigrants, for by so doing some people have shown hospitality to angels" (Hebrews 13:2, NIV).

While we recognize the complexity of immigration laws in various nations, the [church] calls on [Holiness believers] around the world:

- To treat immigrants with love, respect, and mercy.
- To participate sacrificially in local, national, and global compassionate ministry responses to assist refugees and immigrants.
- To encourage their respective governments to approve equitable laws that will allow for family reunification, legal work permits for productive immigrants in the workforce, and pathways for undocumented immigrants to be able to obtain authorized immigrant status.
- To follow the clear biblical mandate to love, welcome, assist, evangelize, and disciple the immigrants near us."[5]

I have been blessed by the global heritage that I received from my parents and my ancestors. A portion of them arrived in Guatemala from other nations and were welcomed by the local people. My parents were always welcomed in the towns where they lived. As a missionary, I have lived in many nations, and I have always been welcomed. I know the feeling of being welcomed in a foreign land. I also know the feeling of being mistreated because of social perceptions and biases toward immigrants—yet the love of a welcoming church by far overshadows the bigotry of a narrow-minded society.

---

5. Board of General Superintendents, Church of the Nazarene, "Statement on Refugees and Immigrants" (November 2015), reprinted in "BGS Echoes Call for Compassion after Latest Refugee Rulings" (January 2017), https://nazarene .org/article/bgs-echoes-call-compassion-after-latest-refugee-rulings.

5

ALMOST
TOO POOR

THE FINAL MOVE my parents made in their process of step migration was to a marginal town on the periphery of Guatemala City. Ironically, the name of this community was El Milagro (The Miracle), a settlement that was built to house poor, working-class people who had migrated from the countryside and needed access to the goods and services of the city. While it was designed with urban development in mind, El Milagro was basically an unplanned slum in the periphery of the city. We moved there when I was eight, and, after living overcrowded in one room, this two-bedroom home felt like a castle. We all thought we had arrived!

El Milagro is a typical slum where the urban poor live. Houses are piped for water and sanitation, but the provision of water is limited to a couple of hours, one day a week, with nearly no pressure. Streets are not paved, and most of the people commute through narrow, crowded alleys. Perhaps they called it "The Miracle" because it was a pure miracle to have water and electricity and public transportation all working at the same time! However, when we lived there, we were happy because we were all together, we owned a house, and everyone could go to school and study to break the cycle of poverty.

Poverty, I discovered, is a relative term. Absolute poverty is not. I learned about relative poverty when living in El Milagro. As the children of the town's post and telegraph chief, we had many things that other, poorer children didn't. I remember sitting at the dinner table with the family and sharing limited meals that rarely included meat or packaged products and seeing my mother often setting a place for an extra person. We were always vying for bread or tortillas or the once-a-week case of sour cream and cheese. As kids, we didn't like it when Mom set the empty place at the table.

"It's for the street kid," she often said. "You have food daily, but those street kids sometimes go to bed with an empty stomach."

How right she was! There were three children from a very poor, working-class family who often knocked on our door and asked for leftovers to eat.

My mother would tell them, "We have no leftovers, but you are welcome to eat with us what we are having today." In this manner we soon discovered that there were people who were even poorer than us.

The public elementary school we attended was named after one of the Catholic archbishops in the country. Mariano Rossell y Arellano had been known for his interest in educating the elites of the country, and he had founded one of the finest private schools in the nation: San Sebastián School, a private Catholic boys' school located in the historic center of Guatemala City. To honor Monsignor Rossell and his interest in education, the government had named our elementary school after him, which proved to be a good thing. Every year, students and teachers from wealthy San Sebastián would visit the "little school in the slum" and bring school supplies, snacks, and a day of recreation for the poor children of El Milagro. In addition, to honor their founder, the administration of San Sebastián created the annual Monsignor Rossell Scholarship for the best student who finished his elementary education in El Milagro. These gifted students were to receive a full-tuition, all-expenses-paid scholarship to complete the six years of secondary education in one of the most prestigious and expensive private schools in the country.

My brother Moises was awarded the scholarship in 1971. Since I attended the same elementary school, my dream was to follow in my brother's footsteps. It seemed unlikely for the scholarship to be awarded twice to the same family, but we were surprised when that was exactly what happened. I received the scholarship in 1974. A daily commute from poverty to wealth and back was about to start.

My years as a student at San Sebastián were filled with paradoxes. Most of my classmates came from some of the wealthiest families in the country. The school followed a strict Catholic system of education for boys, and it was connected to the national archdiocese. Most students were dropped off at the school by their chauffeurs every morning, and some of them were even walked into the facilities by their nannies. All students were required to wear daily, spotless, perfectly groomed uniforms specially tailored by one of the most exclusive stores in the country. On special occasions, students wore gala uniforms, which were replicas of the uniforms from military academies in the United States.

My brother and I observed a slightly different schedule from most of our classmates. We left the slum in El Milagro at five o'clock in the morning to catch the bus that would drop us off twenty blocks from the school. From there, in order to save money for our soft drink at lunch, we would walk for nearly an hour to make it on time for the seven-o'clock start. Classes ran until four o'clock with a one-hour lunch break at noon. My brother and I (and a small number of wealthy students who lived too far away) were the only ones who stayed in the school for lunch. Everyone else followed the same routine: picked up by their chauffeurs or nannies, taken home to eat, and returned on time for the afternoon session. We could say that poverty and exhaustion put us at a major educational disadvantage, but we never knew that was an issue for us. What we did know was that we were being educated in one of the finest institutions of the country, and we felt privileged to be there.

San Sebastián operated on the basis of merit and excellence awards. Historically, only the children of the most influential families in the nation received the school's annual awards. In 1972, however, my brother received his first academic merit medal, and he continued to receive it until he graduated as an educator in 1977. There was another medal—the medal of academic excellence and achievement—that had been awarded exclusively to upperclassmen whose families had significantly influenced the life of the school and the academic status of the institution. Our family was pleasantly surprised when I became the first underclassman ever to be awarded the medal because of my academic performance. I still remember my humble mother sitting in the auditorium and proudly watching her two sons being recognized for their academic performance.

But the daily commute between extreme poverty and extreme wealth took a toll on me. My brother was able to fit well in the culture of wealth that surrounded us, but I simply couldn't cope. I remember being made fun of by some of my classmates because I wore the same shirts and shoes the entire year even though I had outgrown both. I remember being invited to their mansions to spend the night because some parents offered me pocket money in exchange for my tutoring their children who were behind in some of the subjects. These overnight stays proved to be damaging to my soul.

I had grown up attending Protestant churches since my early childhood, and that didn't change during my years at San Sebastián.

However, since it was a Catholic school, Sunday Mass attendance was obligatory for all students. Since we couldn't afford to lose the scholarship, my parents allowed my brother and me to attend early Sunday Mass at our school and then catch the bus to the Landivar Nazarene Church, where our family gathered every week.

The daily commute between poverty and wealth also resulted in a weekly commute between Catholic and Evangelical traditions. This also included times with our classmates who, exposed to the apathy of wealth, exposed us at an early age to the vices of affluence. Soon I found myself staying at my classmates' homes as early as the age of thirteen and partaking with them in partying, smoking, and drinking. The pressure of the environment, the dichotomy of attending two churches with different faith traditions, and the pressure to fit in a society designed for the wealthy were all too much for me. I was quickly being shaped into a different person—too poor to fit in the high spheres of Guatemala's wealth and too astray to fit in the pious Holiness life of my Nazarene family back home.

Even more pervasive than the literal double life I lived while attending that school, perhaps the hardest thing that caused the most impact in my life as an adolescent was the subtle bullying I received at the hands of some of those students, who, spoiled by their affluent environment, made sure I knew that I didn't really belong with them. Early in my teenage years I learned about the vast inequalities in the world as I journeyed daily between the social and economic extremes of my world.

While my older brother was able to finish high school there, I simply couldn't handle the dualities of my young life. I couldn't sustain the daily commute from poverty to wealth and back; the weekly commute from a Nazarene home to a Catholic environment; and the increasingly regular commute between a pious family life and a personal life of sin and disobedience. I simply couldn't stand the pressure to fit where I didn't really fit.

Poverty and Inequality in the World

By most accounts, poverty has been a complex and misunderstood topic throughout history. On the one hand, every society and culture throughout the history of humanity has had poor, oppressed, and exploited people. The fact that poverty has always existed has made humans navigate around it as something that should be part of our daily lives.

Partially, poverty is misunderstood because we have not been able to distinguish between absolute and relative poverty. Humans have been designed to have their needs met by the resources around them, and any time those resources are unavailable, people suffer. Regardless of culture and tradition, all humans expect to meet their basic needs of food, shelter, and health as part of the human condition. So absolute poverty exists when a social group within the context of larger humanity cannot meet those basic human needs for itself.

Sadly, in a global population of nearly 7.5 billion people, the World Bank determined that in 2015, 10 percent of the world's population (or 734 million people) lived below the global poverty line of $1.90 a day. These people are considered to live in extreme, absolute poverty. However, the problem is deeper when we consider poverty beyond monetary metrics. If we add access to education, sanitation, and security as measures of poverty, the estimation is that nearly 25 percent of the world's population lives in absolute poverty.[1] While the causes of absolute poverty vary, the most widely accepted causes are conflict, exploitation, modern slavery, ethnocentrism, greed, and geography.

Relative poverty is a different concept. Most people in the developed world have not experienced absolute poverty since their economies, governments, and social welfare systems are designed

1. The World Bank, "Poverty," October 7, 2020, https://www.worldbank.org/en/topic/poverty/overview.

to prevent it. Thus, relative poverty is when a number of people in a given society have significantly less access to the goods, services, and wealth of the average person in that society. The higher the development of a society, the lower the percentages of relative poverty among their people.

The complexity of the issue is exacerbated when absolute and relative poverty are placed in the same thinking process. For example, when asked about the causes of poverty in the developed world, many people—including sociologists and economists—blame culture, behavior, laziness, and personal choice.[2] This commonly accepted theory of the causes of poverty in the Western world contrasts with the reality of absolute poverty caused by structural factors in the majority of poor nations in the world. Because of the diametrically opposed views on poverty and its causes, people in the world have also found opposing views on how to deal with it in righteous and humane ways. Sadly, this has also affected whether Christians view poverty as the social evil that it is.

Some of us have grown accustomed to having poor people around us, and we have found ways to respond to poverty. Some simply choose to ignore the plight of the poor. Others have found means to respond to poverty by giving alms and donations so that those who work to alleviate poverty can continue their mission. Others go as far as working with and for the poor in changing the unjust structures that have caused fellow humans to live in conditions below the dignity of God's creatures. What is the foundation for such difference?

First of all, we need to recognize what type of poverty we are addressing. Absolute poverty can be addressed through means that target either alleviation or elimination. When my mother went every Tuesday to the distribution center that Caritas (the charitable arm of the Catholic Church in Guatemala) had opened close to our home in

---

2. Christopher A. Sarlo, "The Causes of Poverty," Fraser Institute, 2019, https://www.fraserinstitute.org/sites/default/files/causes-of-poverty.pdf.

Mixco, she gratefully received the help they put together to alleviate our condition of urban poverty. Without their biweekly donations of food, our family wouldn't have been able to manage the basic needs we had to feed a large number of children.

Poverty *elimination*, however, is a deeper exercise. It requires changes in societies that result in macroeconomic growth, access to economic opportunities, development of social services at every level, reduction of illiteracy, reduction of child mortality, wider promotion of opportunities, increased security, and preservation of the environment and the means of production. The road to poverty elimination is so long that most societies prefer to work on alleviating poverty rather than eliminating it.

In an environment of wealth and social development, the issue of poverty is different. Many of us currently live in societies where we witness relative poverty. There are still pockets of people who suffer from nutritional deficiencies, unemployment, lack of accessible healthcare, and equal opportunities. The fact that this happens in the context of wealth doesn't take away the reality of poverty. But in cases of relative poverty, the answers are different. Relative poverty is addressed either by an increase in social services or increased emphasis on social equality and justice. Again, the provision of social services seems to be the faster, more preferred route to the deeper journey toward social equality and justice.

As if the pernicious impact of poverty in the life of an individual were not enough, poverty has often been used as a mechanism to further isolate and reject people from the core of society. Poverty by itself excludes people from development and growth opportunities that present themselves to the majority of people. And society has made it so that the poor are further excluded by virtue of their own condition, exacerbating their lack of access to means and opportunities to break the cycle of poverty. This is one of the reasons Jesus came—to highlight the plight of the poor and proclaim release from the ever-oppressive cycle of poverty that traps many people in the world today.

What Does the Bible Say?

I remember one of the first seminars on poverty alleviation that I gave overseas during my early years as a trainer. As I challenged the participants to mobilize the church to be the healing hands of Jesus for the poor, a well-intentioned missionary told me that our social work was a distraction to the evangelizing work of the church. He went on to say, "Jesus himself reminded us that the poor will always be with us." His argument was that, since the poor will always be with us, we should basically stop trying to solve the problem of poverty and focus on evangelism instead.

I couldn't disagree more. The reality of the gospel is that it is *good news* for the whole person in the whole world. While it is true that Jesus rebuked the disciples' false solidarity when he was anointed in Bethany in what they thought was a waste of money that could have been given to the poor, Jesus was not making light of the reality of poverty, oppression, and exploitation. The disciples were simply putting things out of context in God's kingdom. What Jesus told them was that a true act of mercy and justice cannot be done in isolation from him, the very source of justice and righteousness. Additionally, from his declaration of mission in Luke 4 to his description of the end times in Matthew 25, Jesus placed the poor at the center of his mission, his message, and his ministry.

In fact, I venture to say that the poor had a special spot in Jesus's heart. The incarnate God called his disciples to see him in the poor, the hungry, the stranger, the prisoner, the sick (Matthew 25:31–46). He challenged the religious practices that were high on religiosity and void of solidarity with and compassion for the poor and dispossessed. His message to the disciples in Matthew 25 was his contemporary recitation of the message given to the people through the word of the prophet Isaiah:

Is not this the kind of fasting I have chosen: to loose the chains of injustice and untie the cords of the yoke, to set the oppressed free and break every yoke? Is it not to share your food with the hungry and to provide the poor wanderer with shelter—when you see the naked, to clothe them, and not to turn away from your own flesh and blood? Then your light will break forth like the dawn, and your healing will quickly appear; then your righteousness will go before you, and the glory of the LORD will be your rear guard. Then you will call, and the LORD will answer; you will cry for help, and he will say: Here am I.

(Isaiah 58:6–9a)

It is interesting that, in this rebuke to the religious symbolism that is void of solidarity and compassion, the Lord is encouraging us to address both absolute *and* relative poverty. He is asking us to do both alleviation, by sharing our resources, *and* justice, by speaking on behalf of the poor, the oppressed, and the marginalized. The message of Jesus was one of restoration—restoration of God's people with their Creator and restoration of God's people to a full life the way God intended.

The church where Mom and Dad met Jesus was a church that not only preached but also *demonstrated* God's love for everyone. It was a church that went to be with the poor. It was a church that incarnated itself with the poor. And it was also a church that, since its beginnings, had been established to minister to and embrace the poor. That's why I was thankful when that denomination's stance in favor of the poor became part of the official polity of the church:

Responsibility to the Poor. [We] believe that Jesus commanded his disciples to have a special relationship to the poor of this world; that Christ's church ought, first, to keep itself simple and free from an emphasis on wealth and extravagance and, second, to give itself to the care, feeding, clothing, and shelter of the poor. Throughout the Bible and in the life and example of Jesus, God identifies with and assists the poor, the oppressed, and those in society who cannot speak for themselves. In the same way, we too are called to identify with and to enter into solidarity with the poor and not simply to offer charity from positions of comfort. We hold that compassionate ministry to the poor includes acts of charity as well as a struggle to provide opportunity, equality, and justice for the poor. We further believe that the Christian responsibility to the poor is an essential aspect of the life of every believer who seeks a faith that works through love.

Finally, we understand Christian holiness to be inseparable from ministry to the poor in that holiness compels the Christian beyond his or her own individual perfection and toward the creation of a more just and equitable society and world. Holiness, far from distancing believers from the desperate economic needs of people in our world, motivates us to place our means in the service of alleviating such need and to adjust our wants in accordance with the needs of others.[3]

---

3. Church of the Nazarene, *Manual: 2017–2021*, 394.

6

ALMOST ENLISTED

I LEFT MY PARENTS' HOME for a second time at the age of fourteen. This time I wanted to experience what my other siblings had experienced—not because of economic limitations but because of a personal choice. So I asked my parents if I could withdraw from the scholarship I had at San Sebastián and go to the interior to finish high school at a dorm while learning a trade. Since my other siblings had already done that, the request didn't come as a surprise to my parents.

It was 1978, and Guatemala was in the middle of a civil war. It had already been more than two decades since the coup d'état that had overthrown the last democratically elected president, and the country was ruled by military dictatorship. The tension between the world's superpowers in the second half of the century had found a battleground in Guatemala. Almost every family was affected by the civil war, and we were no exception.

Within months of my arrival at the German Technical Institute in Mazatenango in the south of Guatemala, I was already part of a group of students who were being indoctrinated by some college professors and university students in town who were part of the revolutionary movement in Guatemala. The norms of the dormitory in my school were that students would visit their homes every other weekend while spending the off weekends in town. That weekend in town became critical in my indoctrination process, since I spent time learning the intricacies of Maoism while reading and studying in detail Chairman Mao's *Little Red Book*.

The plan was simple yet effective. Every Saturday a trainer met a group of ten or so high school students in various locations. We never knew the name of the instructor, but we always knew the place where we were supposed to meet him, every other Saturday in a different location. We met under trees, under bridges, or in the forest. Anywhere was fair game as long as the meeting place was remote and we could know when someone was approaching. We read the book with much attention, and the case studies of the Cultural Revolution appealed to a group of intellectually motivated teenagers seeking an identity of sorts.

My role in the study cell was to be the religious plant. They knew I attended church back home and that I knew some Scripture and Christian songs. In fact, I had been encouraged to get a black leather Bible cover, inside of which I could carry my copy of Mao's *Little Red Book*. As the religious plant, my job was to start leading with songs and to pretend I was giving devotions to the group whenever we were alerted that someone was approaching the area where the cell was meeting. As soon as the threat of discovery disappeared, our instructor went back to Mao's revolutionary teachings.

This continued for more than a year while the civil war in Guatemala intensified. In the meantime, because of my oratory and public-speaking skills, I was soon competing in national speech events, where my name became known in public high school education because of the "revolutionary tone" of my speeches. By the end of 1979, I had been elected vice president of my school's student body, and we organized many political events and demonstrations with the purpose of disrupting the town's life and making a point about the poverty and oppression of the peasants in our country. The themes we promoted and proclaimed were all intended to mobilize young people to support the revolutionary side of the civil war.

One day in late October 1979, as I was heading home from Mazatenango, a town located about a hundred miles from Guatemala City, I was doing what I normally did on the weekends that we were allowed to go home: I left the dorm at one o'clock in the afternoon on Friday and walked to the main road to stand by a gas station and hitchhike my way home. (Most of us hitchhiked because we either didn't have money or wanted to save it. We hitchhiked for several hours until the middle of the afternoon and then got on the last evening bus to ensure we would make it home on time for the weekend with our parents.)

I had made some progress that day—I had managed to get a couple of rides that put me close to the capital city. As I waited for what I hoped would be the last ride of the day, a car stopped right in front of me, and the driver asked me to jump in and get in the front seat with him. He asked if I was going home, and I responded affirmatively. After several minutes of small talk, he got to the point.

"You know that you have made quite a name for yourself among debating high schoolers," he said. "However, you also know that the revolution is not won with little speeches. The revolution is won only when people walk their talk. At this moment, there is no time for people to be engaged in vain discourse. Your name is already on the lists of the country's paramilitary, like the names of hundreds of other students and leaders—who have either been killed or have chosen to join the ranks of the guerrilla." His tone was empathetic.

There was silence in the car for a moment before he continued, with determination, "This is the time for you to make a choice. If you continue exposing yourself publicly in speeches, all you will accomplish is to get yourself killed—and this is not fair to your family. If, on the other hand, you want to put your words into action, I can arrange for you to join the guerrilla movement. A couple of blocks ahead, there is a comrade who, if you get on the back of his motorcycle, will take you to the mountains where some of your classmates have gone and joined the guerrilla. If, on the other hand, you choose not to join the guerrilla, I will drop you off right here, and I urge you to stop participating in public speaking. Lie low, get back to your studies, and forget we had this conversation. I don't want to hear that you were killed."

That conversation put me in a deep quandary. On one hand, I had been indoctrinated for more than a year on the ideological grounds of the Maoist Cultural Revoluton. I had been speaking at nationally known events about the revolutionary movements in Latin America, and I had been elected as a leader of my student body because I represented the ideals of many young people who had witnessed oppression, inequality, and poverty in the country. On the other hand, although I believed that something had to be done, I didn't think the armed struggle was the answer. In a matter of seconds, even though I was not at that time a Christian believer, the many lessons I'd heard from my pious Christian parents and Sunday school teachers began to echo in my head. Something deep inside my heart told me that this was not the reason for which I had been created. I didn't know what that something was, but later I learned that God's prevenient grace was at work in my life and that my parents' prayers were being heard at the throne of grace.

"I can't" was the only thing I could say. I knew something had to be done, but I also knew that you couldn't right a wrong through violence and war. Deep inside I knew I was a pacifist in solidarity with those who suffer. "I can't" was the only thing I could utter. The driver looked at me and paused, expressing without words that he understood my response.

He continued driving as we passed the place where I was supposed to be dropped off to meet my contact. Then he emphatically said, "Then I will say it for the last time. From now on I want you to stop talking privately or publicly about the revolution; I want you to lie low and devote yourself to your studies. I don't want you to get killed for something you are not willing to die for." He drove about a mile past the meeting point, gave me some money to take the bus and go home, and disappeared.

That driver was my older brother Rene. He was a leader in the guerrilla movement in Guatemala, and he was responsible for recruiting and mobilizing new members. I was almost enlisted.

The Tragedy of War

"War is the worst word in the world." This sentence was a tongue twister I learned when I was trying to learn English. Apparently, the combination of consonants is as difficult for Spanish speakers to enunciate as it is for English speakers to roll their Rs. But as difficult as it is to enunciate this sentence, the true difficulty resides in believing it. War is indeed one of the worst things to have ever happened and to continue to happen throughout the history of the world.

Why do people engage in warfare when they can accomplish their hopes and dreams through dialogue and cooperation? The reality is that, as long as humans are selfish, ambitious, greedy, and ethnocentric, wars will always exist as the simplest and most brutal of solutions for accomplishing our goals. War and violence are the tools of bullies and of the weak. It happens in the most basic of environments. In a household, when a member of the family cannot accomplish their wishes through love and dialogue, they may resort to violence. When an abusive husband and father is not willing or able to take the time to converse, to understand, to mediate, and to lovingly persuade, he resorts to violence because it is faster and simpler.

Unfortunately, war never accomplishes what it intends. An occupied land cannot be freed through violent means. Peace cannot be accomplished through violence. The truth is that violence breeds more violence, resulting in centuries-old cultures of violence, revenge, and hatred. This reality has been the history of humanity, and it will unfortunately continue as long as humans are ruled by sin.

I was born and raised in the midst of a civil war. In fact, the recent history of my country is a sad history of occupations for the sake of exploiting the natural resources of the land. Settled by pioneer natives, the region of Mesoamerica has been rich in flora, fauna, and natural resources that explorers have been interested in harvesting. The indigenous tribes of Guatemala were also known for their "warrior spirit" of conquest and occupation. They survived by subduing, enslaving, and ruling over the weaker, unorganized, smaller tribes. In turn, when the colonial explorers arrived in the late 1490s, they used warfare, genocide, and slavery as their tools for harvesting the resources of the land.

By the time of the Guatemalan independence in 1821, the natives had been fully subdued, and peace in the land had been accomplished by what the early Roman Empire termed *Pax Romana*—which was a tense and coerced state of relative peace and stability across the empire, achieved through military intimidation, intervention, and conquest. In other words, a new cultural norm in society had been established, whereby war and military activity became the central component of peaceful living. After Guatemala achieved independence from Spain, life in the newly independent nation was marked by internal and continental wars, which in turn resulted in a culture of violence, occupation, and war in every segment of the population.

By the time I was a teenager, war was part of daily life in Guatemala. One memory I have illustrates this grotesque reality perfectly. Later in life, when I was a young architect, my company was part of an Independence Day celebration with a church-sponsored orphanage that we had designed and built. At the celebration, the two most active and involved children at the orphanage were invited to raise the flag to mark the opening of the festivities. Sadly, both children's parents had been killed by each other's enemy in the civil war. One kid's father was a drafted member of the military, while the other kid's father was an enlisted member of the guerrilla army. The legacy of civil war in my country had left orphans, widows, and destruction in its wake.

Sadly, just like the conflict-ridden history of Guatemala, the history of the rest of the world is also marked by periods of war and civil struggle. The biggest markers of human civilization and the biggest shifts in human history can be traced back to the devastating events prompted by wars. In fact, there has not been a single period in the history of the world that has not been affected by war somewhere on the planet. This was true in the past, and it remains true today. In the first two decades of the twenty-first century, for example, the post-9/11 warzones of Iraq, Syria, Afghanistan, Yemen, and Pakistan have caused more than an estimated 800,000 casualties.[1] This number doesn't even take into consideration the more than 25 internal, continental wars that happened around the world during the same period.

While wars certainly take a significant toll on the warring factions, the reality is that wars cause additional damage and casualties among civilians and other vulnerable people who get caught in the middle. For example, the same study of post-9/11 casualties estimates that 335,745 of those killed in global conflicts were civilians, amounting to roughly 42 percent of the total death toll. Further, of the large number of civilians and vulnerable people directly impacted by the darkness

---

1. Niall McCarthy, "The Death Toll of Wars Since 9/11," Statista, February 4, 2020, https://www.statista.com/chart/20699/estimated-number-of-deaths-in-selected-warzones/.

of war, children and youth are the ones who are most impacted in both the long and short term. The catastrophic impact of war is exponentially magnified in the lives of children and youth in terms of their survival, development, and well-being. One of the darkest tragedies of war is that, throughout history, children have been both innocent casualties of armed conflicts *and* involuntary recruits into military roles without proper development or training.

I have had the privilege to visit multiple war-ravaged nations in order to provide assistance on behalf of the church. Whether it was the killing fields of Rwanda or refugee camps in Jordan, Côte d'Ivoire, Congo, Mozambique, Kenya, Algeria, or the West Bank, the pattern of loss was the same. Innocent families with their children had been displaced from their homes by the brutality of war. Their plans had been cut short and their dreams shattered. I saw how children were both afraid of war while at the same already preparing for it. Adults had forced innocent children into a pervasive culture of war and violence. It doesn't have to be that way.

What Does the Bible Say?

God designed the world to live in harmony. The original design of humanity was to live in harmony with itself and with the rest of God's creation. This concept of complete harmony and wholeness is known in the Old Testament as *shalom*, which most of us simply translate as "peace." Yet the biblical concept of *shalom* transcends this simple translation, and furthermore, the concept of peace is also more complex than we typically allow. Peace is not merely the absence of conflict. Peace is the absence of the *conditions* that give birth to conflict. Peace is restoration of the original state of harmony, wholeness, and justice that God intended for creation. Peace involves the elimination of the circumstances and evil that give birth to the tensions and wars in the world so that people can enjoy the original state of harmony for which God created us. This all-encompassing sense of *shalom* is described throughout Scripture from Genesis to

Revelation. "God saw all that he had made, and it was very good" (Genesis 1:31a). "'He will wipe every tear from their eyes. There will be no more death' or mourning or crying or pain, for the old order of things has passed away" (Revelation 21:4).

Peace is not achieved through oppressive means. When God came to the earth in the person of Jesus, he didn't come to establish peace through another version of *Pax Romana*—a peace that was forced on people through the oppressive instruments of military violence and intimidation. When Jesus introduced true peace to his disciples, he made sure they understood that his peace was not like the peace the world offers, for the peace of this world is often conditional, manipulative, and forced upon us through either subtle or obvious means of oppression and deceit (John 14:27).

True peace is a state of hope in the midst of conflict. True peace is a sense of certainty in the midst of fear. True peace is a sense of calm in the midst of the storm. It transcends the circumstances and helps us change the circumstances by allowing us not to be trapped by them. Even after his resurrection, when the disciples gathered in seclusion—for fear of those who had threatened to kill them as they had done to Jesus—the Lord appeared to them and reminded them of the true sense of peace. "Peace be with you" was the gift they received in the midst of their fear (John 20:19, 21). These words reminded them of the restorative power of peace. This is the peace that the apostle Paul referred to when he addressed the church in Philippi from the loneliness of prison. It is a peace that impacts the whole being, bringing back an entire state of wholeness—*shalom*.

With that understanding of peace as *shalom*—true wholeness— the mandate is not to be mere peace lovers. We must be peace*makers*, even in the midst of our circumstances. God's instructions for people in exile were not only to live in peace with one another and with their oppressors but also to "seek the peace and prosperity [*shalom*] of the city to which I have carried you into exile" (Jeremiah 29:7a). This has been God's design ever since the fall of humanity—for creation to be actively procuring and promoting the restoration of harmony, wholeness, and prosperity. *Shalom* on earth. That's why Jesus called peacemakers "blessed" with the most precious symbol of blessing: God's adopted character in us. When Jesus called a blessing upon the peacemakers, his promise was that, as we seek the peace and prosperity of the communities and societies where we are planted, we will display the essence of the character of God as God's children: "Blessed are the peacemakers, for they will be called children of God" (Matthew 5:9).

I once had the opportunity to meet Billy Mitchell. Billy had been a leading member of the loyalist paramilitary during the years of armed conflict in Ulster (United Kingdom). He was given a life sentence for his role in a feud that resulted in the murder of two individuals. During his time in prison, Billy—a nominal Protestant from Belfast—entered into a personal relationship with Christ in 1979. He renounced his paramilitary membership and joined peacemaking efforts from prison. In the meantime his wife, Mena, had been ministered to by a Christian group in town, and together they decided to live a life of Christ-centered peacemaking. While in prison, Billy started reaching out to prisoners from both camps in the conflict. They were separated by fences, and he decided to first promote peacemaking among those in his camp and then approach the prisoners from the other side of the fence with a message of peace and reconciliation.

In 1990, Billy was released from prison, and he continued his personal quest to mobilize warring factions toward the cause of peace. By the time I met him in 1994, he had been actively involved for several years in "conflict transformation" with the purpose of bringing peace, reconciliation, and change in society so that people could live in harmony with one another while eliminating the core causes of injustice, hatred, and division. It was my honor to be with Billy in November 1994 at Belfast City Hall, where the Lord Mayor of Belfast bestowed him with the Peacemaker's Honor.

The Wesleyan tradition is a peacemaking tradition. In his sermon about the Sermon on the Mount, John Wesley defined peacemakers:

Hence we may easily learn, in how wide a sense the term peace-makers is to be understood. In its literal meaning it implies those lovers of God and man who utterly detest and abhor all strife and debate, all variance in contention; and accordingly labor with all their might, either to prevent this fire of hell from being kindled, or, when it is kindled, from breaking out, or, when it is broke out, from spreading any farther. They endeavour to calm the stormy spirits of men, to quiet their turbulent passions, to soften the minds of contending parties, and, if possible, reconcile them to each other.[2]

---

2. John Wesley, "Sermon 23: Upon Our Lord's Sermon on the Mount: Discourse Three," The Wesley Center Online, http://wesley.nnu.edu/john-wesley/the-sermons-of-john-wesley-1872-edition/sermon-23-upon-our-lords-sermon-on-the-mount-discourse-three/.

7
ALMOST
TARGETED

I RELUCTANTLY HEEDED my brother's advice to stay quiet and avoid any type of leadership involvement in my high school. I was sixteen when I entered my final year of high school. Academically, everything was fine, but my personal life was more influenced by the political indoctrination and erratic behavior of dorm life than by the lessons I had learned at home and at church growing up. The school principal warned my mother and me about my involvement in student government, and he allowed me to enroll in school on the condition that I would stay away from political activism. With regard to my spiritual life, church was a convention I agreed to during the weekends that I visited home twice a month, but I hadn't made a decision for Christ.

When I graduated from my technical high school, I was recruited to work for a German communications firm in the capital city. I decided to take a year off from studying to devote myself to work and to practice the trade I had learned at school. In the meantime, the country continued to be submerged in a civil war that had taken tens of thousands of lives, affecting nearly every family in the country. My family was no exception.

By the end of 1979, my older brother Rene was fully engaged in the guerrilla movement and had reached the high ranks of leadership thanks to his ideological and strategic acumen. He had graduated as a medical doctor and joined the guerrilla while doing his residence as a pediatrician in the national hospital in the capital city. In the process, he married one of his colleagues, who was also a medical doctor and a family friend. After their wedding they moved to Tactic, a small town close to Cobán, where my brother was responsible for recruiting and organizing a large guerrilla cell in the north of the country.

In the meantime, I was living in the city, away from any political involvement, as recommended by my brother. Our lives seemed to be tranquil and unaffected by the civil war until one day, on the first anniversary of my brother's wedding, a relative of his wife's leaked to them the information that his name was on the list of those who were going to be assassinated that very day. It was all part of military and psychological warfare. The paramilitary in the country had decided to hit not only my brother but also his extended family. As an anniversary gift, they were planning to target him so that both families—his and his wife's—would be reminded to stay away from dissent and revolutionary activity.

To my brother's fortune, he was alerted on time. On the morning of August 24, 1980—his first wedding anniversary—he fled to neighboring Honduras, from where he was then transported to Nicaragua, Costa Rica, and finally Mexico, where he settled as a formal exile. His wife and three-month-old son were spared and joined him several months later. They still live there today. My sister-in-law tells me that the paramilitaries indeed showed up on August 24 at their clinic in Tactic and searched the entire place for my brother and for evidence that he was engaged with the revolutionary forces in Guatemala. They couldn't find anything, and they left with the warning that it was not over yet.

A year later, our family was still shaken by the reality that my older brother was in self-imposed exile to protect his life. We found ways to continue with our normal lives in the middle of the tension and the ongoing civil war. I continued working for the German firm and started cultivating my dream of moving to Germany to study electronics and engineering. My German bosses encouraged me to study German and to apply to universities there. And then everything changed August 24, 1981.

I had left home with my brother Moises early in the morning on August 24. We didn't even remember that this day was the two-year anniversary of our older brother's wedding and the one-year anniversary of his departure to exile. Our lives were as normal as they could possibly be in the middle of a fifteen-year-old civil war. On our way to work, Moises drove me by the house he had just purchased because he was engaged to marry his girlfriend, Patty, in October of that year. He wanted to show me the house because I had just finished for them a pastel-colored painting of a horse—his favorite animal. We looked at the place where they planned to hang the painting, and I agreed to frame it later that week. Then he drove me to a place where I could catch the bus to work.

Monday, August 24, 1981, proceeded like any other day. I finished my tasks at the shop and visited a couple of clients, and I even took the time to visit with a friend who was about to travel overseas. I took my customary mode of public transport home and arrived at El Milagro, as expected, for dinner at about seven o'clock. However, there was something different in the alley when I arrived. My dad was waiting for me, and I had never seen him so distressed in my entire life—not even at the news of my brother's sudden departure to safety in exile.

"Moises," he said with a broken voice. "They have shot and killed Moises. His body is at the morgue, and we have to go and identify him. Please stay inside and don't go out for any reason. They may try to go after the whole family."

When my parents arrived at the morgue, they had to confirm what no parent would ever want to confirm: that their innocent child had been killed by paramilitary hitmen in the streets of Guatemala. August 24, 1981.

There was a lot of confusion at home. We couldn't put all the pieces together to realize that the strategy of psychological warfare and intimidation extended to every member of my family. We later learned that the assassins had been given instructions to kill one of Rene's siblings as bait so that Rene would return to the country and they could then kill him. We also learned that they used the very special dates in my brother's life to remind him they had complete control of information about him. He married on August 24, 1979. He was supposed to be killed on August 24, 1980, but he escaped. Now, on August 24, 1981, his younger brother was killed at the young age of twenty-two as a dark reminder for the rest of his life. Moises had been driving on one of the main roads of Guatemala City when two men in a motorcycle approached him while a yellow pickup truck moved in front of him to slow him down. In a matter of seconds, they shot his head, his neck, and his heart. He lost control of the truck and ended up on the roadside, dead—on his older brother's second wedding anniversary.

Rene didn't attend Moises's funeral. We all hoped he would stay in exile, and he did. The paramilitary would have wanted to use the funeral as a trap to kill Rene. As my mother used to say, "I have lost one son to this senseless violence, and another is in exile already. We cannot afford to lose another child."

After Moises's assassination, our lives went on a dark downward spiral. That's when I witnessed the strength of my family's faith in Christ and the love of the church. Their church family came alongside my parents and became their source of support. In the middle of all the grief and loss, my parents continued to be faithful to the Lord and to the church. They didn't lower their guard, and they encouraged us to remain vigilant and to be careful with our daily routines. Nobody was safe anymore. There were many instances when we knew that the entire family was under strict surveillance.

One morning, several months after my brother's assassination, my mother came back home from the market in El Milagro. She was unusually stressed out and restless, and we had to pressure her to tell us what was wrong. By now, anything abnormal got our attention. "I just met a man two blocks from here," she said. "He told me he was the one who killed Moises and that he was there to check on the family." He even taunted her and asked if she was planning to do anything with the information she had. He was making sure she and the entire family were intimidated. In the midst of corruption and lawlessness, my mother felt helpless. My brother Freddy and I, however, decided to chase after the man who had admitted to killing my brother.

"Don't go," said my mother. "I have already forgiven him, and I only pray he finds the forgiveness that only Christ can give." She repeated to us that she had already lost two sons—one to exile and one to death—and that she was not about to lose two more.

Several of the records of the infamous civil war in Guatemala were declassified after the peace agreement was signed on December 29, 1996. Journalists and investigators found files that contained tens of thousands of pages with individual information from everyone who, regardless of age, had been involved in either side of the civil war. There were names of those who joined the guerrilla movement and those who were part of the civil rights movements. There were names of those who had been part of the civil disobedience and the student-led movements. Our names were on the files. Instead of Moises, it could have been me.

Political Assassinations as a Tool of Evil

As I was finalizing the writing of this book, I learned that in Russia, Alexei Navalny—one of the most prominent opposition leaders in the country—was the victim of attempted murder through poisoning in an effort to eliminate him as a political competitor.[1] Unfortunately, while this attempt made global news, the reality is that countries and societies are hit daily by the practice of murder for political or other reasons.

One of the most devastating features of a culture of violence caused by war and politics is the justification of political assassination as a way to eliminate, intimidate, or subdue the opposition. Unfortunately, this practice has been deemed not only appropriate but has been especially promoted in places where dialogue and peaceful opposition are not allowed. The numbers of political assassinations in the world are staggering.

Political strategists, policymakers, military strategists, and even dictators consider political assassinations an acceptable practice to eliminate dissent and change the course of history. For example, Jones and Olken's 1875–2004 study on the effect of political assassinations found out that these actions have been a persistent feature of the political landscape throughout history. "From Julius Caesar to Abraham Lincoln, from John F. Kennedy to Yitzhak Rabin, many political leaders have met violent ends—and many others have escaped assassination narrowly."[2]

---

1. Yuliya Talmazan, "Russian Opposition Leader Alexei Navalny Fighting for His Life after Alleged Poisoning," NBC News, August 20, 2020, https://www.nbcnews.com/news/amp/ncna1237413.

2. Benjamin F. Jones and Benjamin A. Olken, "Hit or Miss? The Effect of Assassinations on Institutions and War" (2009), *American Economic Journal: Macroeconomics*, 1 (2): 55–87.

Unfortunately, that was the reality of Guatemala during its thirty years of civil war. According to widely publicized records, "assassination of opposition leaders of the democratic left by so-called death squads, often linked to the military and the police, gave rise to the conviction that [the Guatemalan president] was attempting to eliminate all opponents, whether left, right, or center."[3]

What Does the Bible Say?

Life is God's gift to the human race. Only God has the authority to take someone's earthly life in our journey to eternity. God's commandment "You shall not murder" (Exodus 20:13) is the first commandment that expands from the notion of loving God and family to the laws of peaceful relationships with the community and society at large. It expresses both God's sovereign authority over every human life as well as the sanctity of the lives God created. When an individual decides to terminate another person's life, this individual attempts to take away God's sovereign power to create and terminate life, neither of which has been ascribed to humans.

Although the sixth commandment is one of the shortest in the list of laws given by God to Moses, it is also one of the most relevant in social relations. Almost every society in the world has made this commandment part of its civil and criminal codes. Death by human hands is the single most universal issue that every society faces. In non-civilized societies, murders are the ultimate means of survival, while in highly civilized societies, ending someone's life is still used as a legal instrument to maintain the rule of law (e.g., the death penalty). However, throughout Scripture, God maintains that God is the only one who has sovereignty to end human life. The sanctity of human life is extended to all—born and unborn, rich and poor, law-abiding citizens and criminals, young and old. If Christians be-

---

3. Encyclopedia Britannica, "Guatemala: Civil War Years," https://www.britannica.com/place/Guatemala/Civil-war-years.

lieve that God is the sovereign Creator of all human life, we must also affirm that he and only he has authority to terminate someone's life according to his sovereign will.

It is no wonder that the biblical record of the first murder is immediately followed by God's punishment (even before he gave Moses the law). Abel's murder by Cain's hands was the product of human self-centeredness and jealousy. Cain saw that his own actions were unacceptable to God, who made him aware that sin crouched at the door (Genesis 4:7). Anger and jealousy took control of Cain, who saw his brother's demise as the only way to satisfy his own egotistical desires.

I have often wondered what was in the hearts of those who murdered my brother. I have also pondered what was in the hearts of those who ordered his assassination. The murderers may have been mere agents of a crooked system of oppression, yet their hands were stained by my brother's blood. Both those who ordered the assassination and those who carried it out are guilty—just like Pilate, who washed his hands but consented to the killing of the innocent Christ (Matthew 27:24); just like Saul, who approved of Stephen's stoning (Acts 7:58; 8:1). It was almost me.

8

ALMOST CONDEMNED

I GREW UP ATTENDING CHURCH from the time I was born. My parents were faithful laypeople in every town where we lived, and my dad was frequently elected to the leadership boards in our churches. One could say I was a good church person, but I had not turned my religion into a personal relationship with Christ. I have often said that for many years I was a good Nazarene, but I was not a believer.

During my teen years, after leaving the Catholic school to attend public school, I was far away from the Lord and was leading a double life. I attended church every other Sunday when I was back in town with my parents, but the rest of the days I spent doing things that were not pleasing to God or my parents. I knew the difference, but I willingly and rebelliously acted contrary to what I had been taught. My parents knew about it, but I was too rebellious to listen to them, and we made the agreement that I would please them by attending church on Sunday so they would leave me alone.

Unfortunately, I used the knowledge I had from the Bible and the church for ungodly purposes. Not only was I the "preacher" in the indoctrination cell with my revolutionary friends, but I also joined a group of "religious bullies" who often mocked the small group of evangelical Christians living in the dorm. This handful of young believers had requested permission to have their own room where they could pray and have devotions together without the distractions and emotional abuses of other dorm dwellers, and the school granted their request. However, they were not completely safe because, under the guise of my religious knowledge, I often infiltrated their living arrangements only to create havoc and distraction.

During one of these infiltrations of the young Christians, one of them used a twisted interpretation of Scripture to declare me "eternally unfit for God's saving and redeeming grace." This well-intended and wounded fundamentalist believer used the Bible to tell me I was already condemned and that there was nothing I could do to ever be saved from my sin and rebellion. This pronouncement certainly made me think twice about disrupting life for these believers, but it also left a long-lasting mark in my spiritual life and further search for the saving grace of Jesus.

Months went by, and my rebellious way of life and poor choices were taking a toll on my relationships, both at home and at school. I knew something had to change, but the words that well-intended believer told me made it difficult for me to act on my intuition. I remember coming back from my parents' home to the dorm on a Sunday and feeling the fear of being "Left Behind" when I arrived at the dorm and found it completely empty. The words my Christian classmate had uttered sounded ever so strongly in my head, and I ran to my room convinced that I was condemned and unable to do anything about it.

My search for a meaningful life in the arms of the Lord was long and painful. I attended churches in the area and started reading a lot of books that led me to a deeper soul search. There were times when I quietly sneaked into a church in town to listen to the preaching without the pressure of my family back home, hoping to find the way. Unfortunately, as I tried to make a decision for Christ—whether privately or publicly—the words of that Christian classmate were used by the enemy himself to keep me from finding God's grace and peace. For nearly three years I lived a life of condemnation given to me by someone who had used the Word of God to chastise and dismiss me. Sadly, the longer I searched, the more those words of condemnation found room in my mind and heart.

I graduated from high school and moved back to the city with my parents, and my life as an independent young man took me further away from the church and from any possibility of redemption. So I started reaching into Eastern philosophies and Scientology. To make things worse, one of my closest friends was the son of my parents' pastor in the Nazarene church. We engaged in heavy philosophical dialogue for hours at a time, and we traveled Guatemala together, searching, chatting, and philosophizing about life, spirituality, and church. The thought of salvation was no longer an issue for me, and I felt comfortable with the teachings of Scientology, which—I thought—matched my intellectual search . . . until one day.

After my brother's assassination and a series of other developments in Guatemala's political situation, my friend Eldin left for America for a period of time, and another close friend, Larry, also left the country to go into exile due to political persecution. By then I was deeply immersed in the darkness of grief, loneliness, and desperation. I left my parents' home and moved to a nearby town to live with one of my sisters and her family while attending architecture school. I continued my search but found no answers.

During those days of loss, a former classmate from elementary school reached out to me. Raul had been known as one of the meanest boys in the school. He suffered from polio during his early childhood and had been delayed in his education for many years. So when I was in sixth grade at the age of eleven, Raul was already a fifteen-year-old whose health limitations had made him a bitter teenager who terrorized his much younger classmates.

I had not seen Raul since finishing elementary school and moving on to the private school in the city. So it was a surprise to see him months after my brother's death. It was particularly surprising that he sought me at my parents' home because he wanted to express his sympathy for our family's loss. When we connected, he invited me to play basketball with him. This was an unusual invitation because I had never been athletic, and he had—I thought—a physical limitation. In any case, we played almost every week. Raul traveled to the town where I was living just to play hoops with me, and I appreciated his company.

God's prevenient grace was already at work in my life. Raul had received Christ a couple of years before, and he had a passion to share Christ with those who had chosen to turn their backs to his offer of salvation. Because my dad was the head of the post and telegraph office in our town and because he was a passionate personal evangelist, Raul knew my parents were believers, and he also knew I was beyond being a prodigal. Compelled by the love of Christ, Raul used the excuse of my brother's death to reach out to me and invite me to attend youth camp with him.

I told Raul that I had given up on God. I told him what my well-versed Christian classmate had told me three years before. I told him about my frustration over my brother's death even though my parents were pious followers of Jesus. I shared with him the depth of my exercises in spirituality, and I even encouraged him to join me in the mind-development practices recommended by the Scientology teachers. Nothing seemed to deter Raul from his mission to take me from a seeker to a true follower of Jesus.

The youth camp was organized by the Youth Society of the Central American Mission in Guatemala. It took place during Holy Week of 1983, and God knew I was ready to encounter him. At the closing service on Easter Sunday, after I had heard a convicting sermon the evening before, I heard the Lord's invitation to come to his saving arms. The message that morning was specifically designed to highlight the power of Christ's sacrifice that was enough to atone for any and every sin and human disobedience. The message was clear to my heart, assuring me that nothing, absolutely nothing, could ever keep me from receiving by faith the precious gift of salvation granted through the life, death, and resurrection of Jesus. I rushed to the altar with my hands up as a sign of surrender. I cried with gratitude because the burden of guilt and condemnation had been removed from my shoulders. For the first time in years, I walked without any sense of shame, condemnation, guilt, or fear. I had finally come home!

Easter Sunday has a special meaning for me now because of that experience. I was born anew—like Jesus—on an Easter Sunday. On that special Sunday, I experienced the power of Christ's resurrection and sang the same praises that Peter presented to the believers: "Praise be to the God and Father of our Lord Jesus Christ! In his great mercy he has given us new birth into a living hope through the resurrection of Jesus Christ from the dead, and into an inheritance that can never perish, spoil, or fade" (1 Peter 1:3–4a).

I was reminded that day that, just like death came to humans through one man, Adam, life had also come to God's creation through one man, our incarnate Christ. I was also reminded that day that one man, using God's Word and a twisted theology, made me feel ashamed and condemned while another simple man, with less theology but much love and passion for the lost, ushered me into the path of Christ's saving grace. I was almost condemned by men but was surely redeemed by Christ!

Religious Self-Righteousness and Legalism

I believe that, while sin is responsible for keeping people from a life-giving relationship with God, religious self-righteousness is often responsible for making it harder for people to get to know Christ in his fullness. Self-righteousness and legalism generally get in the way of saving and redeeming grace, in both subtle and overt ways.

In a 2017 study on self-righteousness and morality, Nadav Klein and Nicholas Epley discovered that self-righteousness is not driven by a person's virtues that would deliver them to heaven but by the lesser amount of sins they have so they can freely condemn others by comparison. In other words, self-righteousness based on legalism is not about a person feeling "holier than thou" but rather "less evil than thou."[1] This interesting proposition suggests that self-righteous legalists are more interested in comparing themselves to others than they are with measuring their lives against the light and life of Christ. This revelation is important in understanding the human tendency to condemn others since their condemnation is not based on Christ but mainly on self-developed parameters of morality and behavior.

Condemning others on the basis of self-righteousness is nothing new. In fact, most of the direct chastisements from Jesus to the Pharisees were because of their judgmental, self-righteous behaviors. In fact, Jesus's godly patience was often tested by the Pharisees' attitudes that evidenced their legalism and self-righteousness. He went as far as calling them hypocrites because, in their efforts to justify themselves, they appeared to others as righteous but on the inside were full of judgment, hypocrisy, and wickedness (Matthew 23).

---

1. Nadav Klein and Nicholas Epley, "Less Evil Than You: Bounded Self-Righteousness in Character Inferences, Emotional Reactions, and Behavioral Extremes," *Personality and Social Psychology Bulletin*, June 14, 2017, 1–11.

Steven Cole, in his study of the damning nature of self-righteousness, summarizes five characteristics of a self-righteous person in light of the teachings of Jesus:

1. A self-righteous hypocrite judges the sins of others while overlooking their own sins (Matthew 7:5).

2. A self-righteous hypocrite judges others based on selective standards, not on all of God's Word (Matthew 23:16–21, 23).

3. A self-righteous hypocrite is more concerned about external conformity than with true, inner godliness (Matthew 23:28).

4. A self-righteous hypocrite is not interested in helping others grow in godliness but only on gaining a following (Matthew 23:13, 15).

5. A self-righteous hypocrite justifies themselves by comparing themselves with others or by blaming others for their own sins (Luke 18:11–12).[2]

Having been a Pharisee himself, the apostle Paul knew that self-righteous people have the tendency to justify themselves by blaming others. This is one of the reasons he wrote to the Romans about the damning nature of self-righteousness and legalism: "You, therefore, have no excuse, you who pass judgment on someone else, for at whatever point you judge another, you are condemning yourself, because you who pass judgment do the same things" (Romans 2:1). Judgmental behavior is apparent when seemingly moral people condemn "sinners" even while practicing other, less outwardly flagrant sins. Paul warned of the risk of condemning others for extravagant immorality (Romans 1:23–27), while quietly and intimately partaking ourselves in the relational sins that many of us have been found embracing from time to time (Romans 1:29–31).

---

2. Steven J. Cole, "Lesson 9: The Damnable Sin of Self-Righteousness (Romans 2:1–5), 2010, https://bible.org/seriespage/lesson-9-damnable-sin-self -righteousness-Romans-21-5.

Jo Anne Lyon, a general superintendent emerita for the Wesleyan Church, spoke eloquently about the damning effects of self-righteousness and how it impacts believers particularly. In a 2016 interview, she described herself as a formerly self-righteous person. She "knew everything there was to know" about religion, but she didn't feel good about herself. She was a pastor's wife who had learned everything about religion and morals, but she really disliked people—particularly church people! She was good at being a religious person. She did her devotions every morning and attended all the religious events she was expected to attend, but she had a problem: self-righteousness had taken hold of her entire life, and it manifested in arrogance, pride, and distrust—until one day when, reading a book given to her by her husband, she realized the depths of her self-righteousness. However, she didn't think she needed to confess. In her words, "This is real self-righteousness, at its worst." Her religious self-righteousness had put her in a position where she felt justified in practicing her religion while judging those around her. Fortunately for Jo Anne, that moment of self-evaluation made her "more hungry for God." She went back to the same church with the same people she didn't like and was touched by the Holy Spirit in indescribable ways. The judgment and pride she had as a self-righteous person were replaced by love for them. While self-righteousness had made her a judge of others, love made her a reflection of Christ to them.[3]

What Does the Bible Say?

Self-righteousness wants to keep people out of the kingdom of God, but the good news of the gospel is that God loved us so much that he sent his only Son, Jesus, so that—no matter the depth and

---

3. Jo Anne Lyon, "My Movement from Self-Righteousness to True Holiness," Seedbed, December 17, 2016, https://www.seedbed.com/the-movement -from-self-righteousness-to-true-holiness/.

breadth of our sins—we all can find salvation through his loving atonement, death, and resurrection. Because of the love of Christ, we are never too sinful or too distant to be reached and saved.

Just like the people of Israel, who confessed their sins and found mercy and forgiveness after they had sinned and fallen away from relationship with God, people today can experience the same forgiving love of Christ in their lives. The people of God were reminded that, despite their sins, God had not deserted or abandoned them. They found compassion, love, and forgiveness when they chose to turn from their ways and turn toward God. The same is true for anyone who comes to the Lord today!

The promise that God gave his people through the prophet Isaiah was the same promise that he gave the church through the apostle Paul. "There is now no condemnation for those who are in Christ Jesus" (Romans 8:1). And there is nothing—absolutely nothing!—that can separate us from the saving, embracing, transforming love of Christ. Nothing and no one can bring any charges against those who have been justified by the love of Christ. In fact, like Paul, "I am convinced that neither death nor life, neither angels nor demons, neither the present nor the future, nor any powers, neither height nor depth, nor anything else in all creation, will be able to separate us from the love of God that is in Christ Jesus our Lord" (Romans 8:38–39). And this all-embracing love that expels and nullifies any form of condemnation is the essence of the gospel.

9
ALMOST
FORGOTTEN

ACCEPTING THE GIFT OF SALVATION by grace and faith in Jesus Christ has been the best decision I have ever made. It changed the course of my life completely. I was nineteen years old with a long exposure to and understanding of the Christian faith, but now I had made the journey and experience mine. On one hand, I was tempted to feel disappointed that I had wasted so many years walking away from the Lord and running in circles with no end in sight. On the other hand, I was simply thankful I had made the decision for Christ.

I returned to school after the Easter break that April of 1983. Things were different for me. It was almost unexplainable, but I didn't want to have anything to do with the lifestyle I had led before my encounter with Christ at the youth camp. I wanted to tell someone, but my peers at college were people I partied with, and they didn't want anything to do with Christianity and new life in Christ. However, I decided to go early to school that Monday and to sit on my usual bench.

While I sat there on a virtually empty campus, I heard the voice of one of my classmates who was almost never early to school because he lived a couple blocks away from campus. Stuardo was the son of one of the former undersecretaries of education for my country, and he was known for his Christian witness on campus. "What are you doing here so early?" he asked. Then he went on to say that, as he was doing his morning devotions, he had been prompted by the Holy Spirit to "go early to school to pick up someone he was supposed to disciple." His obedience started a journey and a friendship that has only been strengthened over the years.

Stuardo was active at Central Presbyterian Church in downtown Guatemala City. He was a member of the youth group, a contemporary gospel quartet, and the youth choir. He was more interested in discipling others than he was in architecture school. Helping others grow in the faith was his priority. He was obedient to the prompting of the Lord that morning and went early to school and found me. He invited me to his home, and for months he patiently discipled me, listening to my questions and helping me channel my desire to play guitar and sing so I could use those talents for the Lord.

Even though I became part of the group of Christian college students who met at Stuardo's home for Bible study and discipleship, I didn't join his Presbyterian church. I re-engaged with my home church, where my parents attended, which had a history of leadership development and missional work. When I returned, they didn't even realize I had left since I had continued my sporadic attendance while hiding my double lifestyle.

It was May 1983, and I was on fire for the Lord. I really wanted to make up for lost time, so the first thing my friend told me was that I needed to be baptized in order to serve in my local church. He didn't want to take me away from my religious roots. I soon asked my pastor—who was also my friend Eldin's father—to include me in the next baptismal service.

Don Arnoldo, as we dearly called him, was our pastor. Rev. Arnoldo Juarez was an eloquent preacher who had been trained in the Verapaz region of the country, both as a schoolteacher and as a minister. He was very relational, and the church loved him and his family dearly. I spent most of my days at the parsonage because of my friendship with Eldin. So I was trained almost daily in the nuances of faith, discipleship, rituals, and more.

I was so ready to be baptized. The date neared, and I let my family know that Sunday, May 29, was the date set for my baptism. It was one of the largest baptismal classes in our church, and we were all excited about it. The time had come for me to be enabled to serve according to the traditions of my church, which required workers to be baptized before serving.

Sunday came, and I was ready. I went to Sunday school but was eager for class to end. Then church began, and our pastor announced the baptismal service. He called each candidate by name, and one by one each candidate gave a testimony and was baptized—except for me. The pastor had never called my name! I was embarrassed and ashamed. The words of condemnation from my high school classmate came back to mind. I had been left out.

At the end of the service I pondered the best way to talk to my pastor. He was my friend's dad. I had been in his house at least a couple of days the week prior, but he hadn't called me to be baptized. Was it because I had been discipled by a Presbyterian? I figured there must be a reason I had been excluded from such an important ritual in the life of our church. I asked, "Don Arnoldo, why didn't you call me to be baptized today?"

"Tavito!" he said (my nickname was "Tavo," and adding "-ito" to the end of it signaled endearment). "How could I forget you? You were at the top of my head! But, because we added you to the list so recently, it must have just fallen off. I am so sorry. I didn't mean to forget you. Next Sunday we will baptize you. I promise."

This was good enough for me. I knew he hadn't meant to harm me by unintentionally leaving me out of the baptismal service. I told my family and decided to wait for the following Sunday.

The Tuesday after the forgotten baptism, I was getting ready to go to work when I heard the phone ring. My dad answered and received the news that, while driving with his brother to their native Rabinal in the north-central part of Guatemala, our pastor, Rev. Arnoldo Juarez, had died in a truck accident the previous evening— Monday, May 30, 1983. Our church was devastated! My friend's family was devastated. We had lost one of the most anointed preachers and shepherds of the Church of the Nazarene in Guatemala. A gifted minister had been called to the presence of the Lord, and everyone was impacted by the loss.

In the midst of all the confusion and the loss, something quiet was happening in my heart. I had been forgotten at the baptismal service. I wanted my pastor to baptize me, and he had promised to do so the following week. Did that mean the Lord had forgotten me too? These thoughts germinated quickly in the mind of a brand-new believer. However, in the grand scheme of things, I knew this was not a time to think about myself. I talked to my friends, who recommended I wait for God's time.

Several months went by, and our church had appointed Rev. Juarez's widow to be our interim pastor. She had been trained with him in our Bible school in the north of the country but, for reasons I still don't comprehend, had been discouraged from pursuing ordination. Therefore, she was allowed only to preach and perform administrative functions for the church but no sacraments, including baptism.

The year 1983 was an important one in the history of the global Nazarene denomination. It was the year of the Diamond Jubilee (seventy-five years) for the Church of the Nazarene, and all the churches in the world were planning to join the October celebration, which included celebrating new members. Since in many of the older missionary works, baptism was deemed a requirement for membership, our pastor, Mrs. Juarez, asked me if I wanted to be a member to be presented at our Diamond Jubilee.

"Of course!" I said. "I have been waiting for it since April when I became a believer."

She told me I had to be baptized before the official reception of new members in August, and I told her my story.

"We won't forget you this time," she promised.

On Saturday, July 2, 1983—five weeks after my scheduled baptism—I was finally baptized in a very intimate service with the district superintendent, Rev. Joel Buenafe, as the officiant, and my pastor and another young believer who was baptized that day as the only other two people in attendance. Some people think the service didn't count since there was not a crowd to witness it, but it counted for the world in my heart! In that intimate ceremony I learned that God had not forgotten me.

God gave me even more than I asked after feeling forgotten. Months after my baptism, we got to welcome a new pastor. As good of a preacher as he was, the greatest gift he brought with him was a beautiful daughter who was my age. Rachel brought joy and beauty to our youth group. Two years after their arrival in our church, I made the second-best decision of my life by asking her to marry me. God didn't forget me! God gave me more than I deserved.

I remember telling this story to a group of colleagues who were with me in Jordan for a leadership conference. I shared the story because we were approaching the site where—according to Scripture and verified by archaeological research—Jesus had been baptized in the Jordan River. We planned to conduct a baptismal service there for the son of one of our missionaries who was with us, and the one officiating the sacrament was my good friend David Busic, who had been invited to be our guest speaker for the meetings. After I told the story, David said to me, "You have already been baptized, but now, would you like the opportunity to declare publicly what happened privately?" He offered to join me in the waters of the Jordan River and thank God for the fact that I was not forgotten. It was a beautiful reminder of God's grace upon my life.

The Impact of Social Exclusion and Isolation

Humans were created to live in community. "We are made with a yearning for connection with others at the core of our being. That yearning is ultimately fulfilled as we live in covenanted relationship with God, the creation, and loving one's neighbor as oneself. Our creation as social beings is both good and beautiful. We reflect the image of God in our capacity to relate and our desire to do so. The people of God are formed as one in Christ, a rich community of love and grace."[1]

In general terms, socialization and community allow individuals the ability to access the networks and resources around them so they can enjoy the fullness of life for which they have been created. This gives individuals a great deal of opportunity. Sadly, not everyone enjoys community and belonging that afford them a sense of wholeness. Some people, of course, choose to isolate themselves. But there are larger numbers who end up being pushed or relegated to the periphery of their social construct, whether by circumstance or by socially designed condition. When that happens, those individuals are prevented from having access to those means for which they have been created.

1. Church of the Nazarene, *Manual: 2017–2021*, 54–55.

To make matters worse, humans have a natural tendency to exclude people on the basis of their own sense of belonging and rights. As a result, those who remain in the core of the society develop mechanisms to push people on the periphery even further away. And because of our mechanisms of self-preservation, we create (sometimes intentionally, sometimes unintentionally) concentric circles of belonging where those at the core share the norms, ethos, and thinking of the majority, while those on the fringes differ and have been pushed away as a result. Notably, sometimes people choose to be on the fringes, but most people end up there because they have been pushed out of the core through a subtle (and at times unintentional) process of social exclusion or isolation.

The end result is that those on the periphery are first excluded, then forgotten, and ultimately expelled from the core. At that point the world becomes polarized. Those who were excluded from our neatly woven networks end up creating new networks of their own, where their values and views occupy a new core, ready to push others away—hence, perpetuating the cycle of social exclusion.

Religion has not escaped the pernicious effects of the human tendency to exclude and isolate. During the time of Jesus's ministry, it was not only acceptable but was also expected that people would be excluded on the basis of their ethnicity, their disabilities, their lifestyle, or even their work choices. Samaritans were viewed with disdain; the blind and the disabled were banned from entering the temple; publicans and sinners were chastised in public; and tax collectors were anathema. All lived on the margins of society. Gloriously, Jesus came to minister to and to welcome all of them (see Matthew 9:11; John 4; 5:1–15).

What Does the Bible Say?

I was recently interviewing a candidate for ordination, and I asked him about his conversion story. What he said reminded me of the sense of hopelessness that I experienced when I was almost condemned, then almost forgotten in my journey to join the community of faith. He told me, however, that the church was where he found himself being embraced. He had been forgotten by his father, his friends, and his classmates. But when he joined a small church in rural Kentucky, a group of mentors and believers reminded him that he was not forgotten. They reminded him that he was important to God, so therefore, he was important to them. This young man's story and my story are powerful reminders that, even if we are forgotten by people who are supposed to care for us, God has never forgotten us and will never forget us. He said so to his people through the prophet Isaiah: "Can a mother forget the baby at her breast and have no compassion on the child she has borne? Though she may forget, I will not forget you! See, I have engraved you on the palms of my hands" (Isaiah 49:15–16a).

Interestingly, in making his promise to us, God compares his love with the strongest manifestation of human love and commitment that we can understand—the love of a mother. Unquestionably, there is no human love or devotion stronger than a mother has toward her own child. In developed societies, it is estimated that 90 percent of single parents active in their children's lives are women, while only 10 percent are men. These numbers prove that child abandonment is significantly a male problem. That is why God uses the analogy of the powerful love of a *mother*, rather than generically a *parent*. "Can a mother forget her own child?" This is not a rhetorical question. It is an affirmation of the bond of maternal love. God's promise is that his love is even stronger than the maternal bond. "Though she may forget, I will not forget you!" Mothers don't forget. What God is telling us is that his unconditional and sacrificial love is far stronger than the love he created in mothers. "I will not forget you" is the promise of the everlasting love of God that will be with us always, beyond any human love or commitment.

Further, God shows us the depth of his promise never to forget us. He tells his people—you and me—that he has our names *en-*

graved on the palms of his hands. I remember being at a department store and getting ready to pay the cashier. The attendant had on her left wrist a visible tattoo with the name "Zack" in it. I told her it was nice, and she thanked me and said, "I had it done when my grand-baby died six months ago at the age of three. I did it so I will always remember him." She tattooed her grandchild's name on her wrist to symbolize her undying love for him!

Jesus did exactly the same for you and me. The incarnate God allowed his hands to be pierced on our behalf. The depth of God's love for us is such that he pierced our names on his hands so that they will be permanently written in the book of life. We are no longer forgotten!

10

ALMOST REJECTED

RACHEL AND I MARRIED on March 22, 1986. At that time, her father had been appointed as a district superintendent in a pioneer district in the country, and we had invited a young pastor to be our leader. We were the first couple he married in our congregation, and he has been our family pastor ever since. By then I had finished my coursework in architecture school, but I still had to work on my licensure before I could practice as an architect. The Lord blessed us later with our first daughter, Raquel, and months later, I was living the life of a young professional. I opened my own architectural studio, and my alma mater contracted me to teach history of architecture and social architecture. I was also working as a junior high teacher in vocational training, and our family life was busy, fulfilled, and exciting. We had more than we needed, and the years of limitation, isolation, and loneliness were behind us. I was on what I thought was the path to be a faithful layman in our congregation.

At the end of 1988 I was invited by my friend Stuardo's father to work with him for the Undersecretary of Culture of Guatemala and to serve as an architect responsible for a section of the national cultural patrimony of Guatemala at the National Institute of Anthropology and History. This was an exciting invitation! Some of my professors had talked so much about the cultural gem that the institution was and the important role it played in preserving the rich cultural heritage of the nation. Working there was a dream for many professionals, and I didn't hesitate to accept the invitation to start on January 2, 1989. In order to devote myself fully to such an important assignment in my country, I resigned most of my other professional responsibilities. I only kept my role as an associate professor at the architecture school because of my passion for higher education.

January 2 arrived with much anticipation. I had been attending the office of Anthropology and History of Guatemala during November and December to become more familiar with the job. Dr. Colom (Stuardo's father) and I had attended a couple major openings of archaeological museums in the country, and I was growing increasingly excited even though I was young. I was invited to join the other directors at the cabinet table of the Institute. As the head, Dr. Colom was about to start the meeting to officially introduce me. Then politics got in the way.

Before Dr. Colom made the official announcement, one of the members of the Institute's upper echelon interrupted him and challenged my appointment. "How dare you plan to give to this inexperienced architect the responsibility for our historic patrimony? Not only is he young and inexperienced but, worst of all, he is an evangelical Christian. What role does an evangelical Christian have in preserving our Mayan and Catholic architectural and archaeological sites? Does he even respect them?" These arguments may have seemed logical and reasonable, but it turned out they were just an excuse to mobilize the local union to go on strike, ask for the director's head, and replace him with a corrupt leader who, we later learned, was leading a contraband ring that profited from selling archaeological relics to private buyers in Europe and the United States. Apparently, my appointment offered just the excuse they needed to bring chaos into the Institute.

Dr. Colom kept his composure. I could see he intended to challenge the interruptions and continue with my appointment, but I felt that his efforts would be fruitless. I remembered my professors telling me that, as much as this institution was a cultural gem, it was also a regular battleground for the soul of the nation and that, sometimes, corruption had its way. I stood up and recalled the composure and integrity of those young leaders who, like Daniel and his companions in Babylon, decided in their hearts not to be polluted by the idols of their time. I felt the strength of the Lord come upon me as I addressed the professionals around the table.

"Dr. Colom," I said, "I don't believe that you, this honorable institution, or the national patrimony of Guatemala have to go through this unfortunate charade. You and those who examined me for this role know that my desire is to serve only the interests of our beloved nation. You and I know that we can do it with due respect for our history and the legacy of our ancestors, independently of our faith. I also know that my appointment has the potential to be used for ill and ungodly purposes. So I decline your humbling invitation to serve in this position, and I pray that the Lord will protect you from corrupt officials who use their position of privilege to damage our rich patrimony. Please know that you have my utmost respect and support in all endeavors. Thank you."

I shook Dr. Colom's hand, looked at the cadre of corrupt officials, and left the cabinet meeting with my head held high. Then I cried all the way home. Here I was, unemployed, rejected, and misunderstood. I arrived home to my wife and baby daughter and told Rachel everything that had happened. I promised her I was not going to let a job corrupt my heart and my principles. I was reminded of the proverb "Better a small serving of vegetables with love than a fattened calf with hatred" (Proverbs 15:17). She supported me, we cried together, and we made plans to live within our means while I searched for a new job, since I had left almost everything else for the sake of this opportunity.

That evening, as I went to my university to teach, our secretary welcomed me by giving me a note from the School of Pedagogy. Dr. Colom was the dean of that school in the same university, and he wanted to see me. He told me that after I left the Institute, there was a deafening silence in the room. The ringleaders were obviously hoping that he would carry on with the appointment, giving them the excuse they needed to accomplish their evil plans by going on strike and taking over the facility. When I walked out, I left them with no way forward.

Dr. Colom said, "I am sorry that you had to become collateral damage to keep those corrupt officers from doing what they were planning to do. Just remember: God is faithful and just. Thank you."

Things progressed within certain normality after the events of January 2, 1989. A couple weeks later, I was contracted by the national government as a consultant in community development, and I traveled the country, teaching our poor communities to reach sustainability while protecting our environment. I was fully engaged in my new normal. One day in May 1989, however, things changed. This was, perhaps, the meeting that changed the course of my life forever.

Dr. Colom called me again to his office at the university to tell me that the United States Fulbright Commission had announced the invitation for Guatemalan professional scholars to compete for a handful of graduate scholarships in the United States. I had never heard of the Fulbright scholarship. I went home again and talked to

Rachel about the possibility of putting everything on hold in Guatemala while I explored this exciting prospect. Seven months later, after a series of examinations, I was called to the U.S. Embassy in Guatemala for a final interview. Only a handful of those who applied had been chosen to travel to the U.S. to be trained as Fulbright Scholars. I left Guatemala on January 16, 1990, to learn English at Southern Illinois University—Carbondale. After three months I was able to return to Guatemala in May and bring Rachel and Raquel to the U.S. with me. A new journey was about to start.

God used the rejection of a group of people who didn't know me as an instrument to open the door to something new to accomplish his plans and his vision for my life. This was not the only time that I have been rejected in my life. I have experienced rejection both inside and outside the church. But on every occasion, God allowed rejection to plot for me a new course that led to new opportunities, according to his will and his way. At the end of the day, there is no better place to be or office to hold than those that are ordained by God!

Envy and Self-Preservation

What causes people to feel envy? The history of humanity and even the sacred narrative of Scripture include scores of situations where people succumb to the temptation of envy, even among members of the same family. While we understand that those behaviors are considered vile and unwholesome, the reality is that many social settings (including church environments) are affected by them.

In a study about envy in the workplace, for example, Kim Dogan and Robert Vecchio suggest that these emotions result from the loss caused when another individual is granted the outcome that one desires or hopes for themselves, or when a relationship is perceived to be threatened by the addition of another person.[1]

---

1. Kim Dogan and Robert P. Vecchio, "Managing Envy and Jealousy in the Workplace," *Compensation and Benefits Review*, March 1, 2001.

Envy is a weak emotion found in people and societies that struggle with self-preservation. It is true of politics, workplace tensions, family affairs, and even the institutional church. The lower the self-esteem and self-worth that make people feel threatened, the greater the envy. Sadly, these emotions are pervasive in environments beyond the workplace. We find them commonplace in the church and even in close-knit families. Jealousy and envy are both included among the "acts of the flesh" that the apostle Paul listed as affecting the early believers (Galatians 5:19–21).

What Does the Bible Say?

The biblical narrative has scores of stories where envy took over in the lives of entire families and communities. One such story is that of Joseph and his brothers. We find the heart of the story in Genesis 37: Joseph was a seventeen-year-old shepherd who was loved by his father more than the other siblings. While Joseph didn't help his own cause (he often brought his father bad reports about his brothers), his brothers really despised him and were extremely jealous of him. Granted, as Max Lucado eloquently tells it, Joseph "wasn't the easiest guy to live with. He boasted about his dreams and tattled on his siblings. He deserved some of the blame for the family friction. But he certainly didn't deserve to be dumped into a pit and sold to merchants for pocket change. The perpetrators were his ten older brothers."[2]

However, God had a different plan. In the bigger picture of God's redemptive plan, God allowed the envy of Joseph's brothers (and, later, the lies of the spiteful wife of Potiphar) to work out in Joseph's favor and for the benefit of God's people. In spite of the pain inflicted on Joseph by his brothers' acts of envy, and in spite of the deception and lies of the woman who placed him in jail, God's faith-

---

2. Max Lucado, *You'll Get through This: Hope and Help for Your Turbulent Times* (Nashville: Thomas Nelson, 2013), 101.

fulness remained with Joseph as long as he was faithful to the Lord who had full control of his life.

Joseph could have been bitter because of the rejection he suffered from his brothers. He could have been vindictive and responded to them with the same level of spite and rejection that they used to treat him. But Joseph recognized that God's plans are perfect, even when individuals enact harm to those who follow him. In the case of Joseph, his brothers' evil plans were transformed by God into greater plans. First, he recognized that God's sovereignty cannot be trumped by human intervention. "So then, it was not you who sent me here, but God" are his words when he reveals himself to those who sold him into slavery (Genesis 45:8).

Then Joseph surrendered his right to be vindicated. While his brothers were afraid of Joseph's reaction to their envious actions, Joseph recognized that only God had the right to act on what they had done to him. His final answer to them summarizes the heart of a humble leader, who—in spite of the jealousy of his brothers—recognized God's ultimate intentions: "Don't be afraid. Am I in the place of God? You intended to harm me, but God intended it for good to accomplish what is now being done, the saving of many lives" (Genesis 50:19–20).

As I look back at the many times I have been rejected in what I thought were the best plans for my career and personal life, I soon realize God's hand was there, at times showing me a different path and, at times, allowing rejections so that his sovereign plans might be displayed in my life. Rejections, after all, are only forks in the road of the life map that God has traced for us.

"ALMOST MISSED THE CALL

AFTER I FINISHED LANGUAGE SCHOOL in Carbondale, Illinois, Rachel and I took our three-year-old daughter, Raquel, to Cincinnati, Ohio, where I had been offered an additional scholarship for graduate studies in community planning. We had everything well planned before we departed Guatemala. We sold our car, rented out the house that we owned there, sold our furniture and appliances, and planned to return to Guatemala after two years. The idea was to buy a car in the

U.S., add to the savings we had brought to the U.S., and return with a new career, a third language, and a bright future.

God had a different plan, however. When my family arrived in Carbondale, I had already been struggling with culture shock and the trauma of isolation, lack of language skills, and a completely new set of educational systems and values. I didn't expect the changes to impact me as much as they did during my first months in the country. I was about to lose my compass, and I really needed my family to be with me. I remember talking to the Fulbright counselor and asking her if I could bring my family to be with me sooner. Her reply was that I could bring them only after I passed the language proficiency test, and the minimum timeframe for that was six to seven months. The weeks of winter I spent alone in the American Midwest, without any understanding of my surroundings, took a toll on me.

I asked, "If I pass the test in two months, can I bring my family?"

"You can bring them if you pass the test in two weeks! You just have to pass first," she said.

The challenge was on! Four months later, I was on my way to Guatemala to bring my family back with me.

The effort to make it through language school at an accelerated pace, however, took a toll on my emotional and physical stamina. By the time we arrived together in Carbondale, I was spent, and Rachel was incredibly helpful in assisting me to cope with the trauma. To add to the challenge, Raquel had to be taken to the emergency room because of an infection right in the middle of our transition from Illinois to Ohio. The short visit to the ER and the subsequent medical expenses took care of our carefully laid plans literally overnight.

We arrived in Cincinnati on Labor Day weekend of 1990. Our plans had been to get an apartment on campus at the University of Cincinnati and live there for the duration of the program. Because of the financial demands of our transition and the medical expenses we faced, we could no longer afford the college housing. Not knowing the city, the only place we found that we could afford was on the western side of town, close to a public-housing zone of the city. There we were, without furniture, without money, and with a sick child.

On Labor Day in 1990 I ventured onto the streets of western Cincinnati to look for a garage sale to get some inexpensive pieces of furniture. I saw a sign on a post and rushed to the house to see what I could get for our apartment. With my limited English I asked the older man who lived at the advertised address for some furniture, and he told me that the garage sale was already over. I don't know what message my face sent, but he realized I was in dire need. He took me to his basement and had me pick out some basic pieces of old furniture. For me, anything was golden! He sold me several different pieces that would get us started, for only twenty dollars.

I hurried home carrying two of the chairs that were part of a dining set, happy to tell Rachel the good news of my purchase. While walking down the hill from the old man's house to our apartment, I felt embarrassed about carrying a pair of old chairs while, just months ago, I had been one of the most accomplished young professionals in my country. *How embarrassing*, I thought. *If my students at architecture school could see me here, their young professor, carrying used, third-hand furniture for my apartment, they would certainly mock me. What in the world am I doing here?*

As soon as I had that thought, I threw the chairs to the sidewalk, and then I saw my Savior, carrying not a pair of old chairs but a cross—and not to furnish a student apartment but to save me from eternal damnation. The vision of my Lord carrying the cross for me gave me perspective. I sat down and wept. I thanked Jesus for the gift of life, eternal life, and for provisions for today. Then I got up, picked up the two chairs again, and hurried home to tell Rachel about the good man's generosity. The only problem was that we didn't have a car, and we needed a means to transport the rest of our new furniture.

"Let's do what Grandma would do if she were here," Rachel said. "Let's walk up the hill, and if we see a truck parked outside, we can ask them to help us carry our goods, and we'll offer to pay them." We found a lady with her boy getting ready to go out. She agreed to take us to the old man's house, and when we got there we found that, to our surprise, he had already put some of the furniture in the trunk of his car.

"Do you have a church to attend?" the old man asked us. "If not, here is my card. I go to the Baptist church around the corner, and you are welcome to attend."

When we arrived back at our apartment, we unloaded the furniture. Rachel (who had been raised in California and already spoke perfect English) asked the lady how much we owed her for her help.

"I will tell you how you are going to pay me: you will allow me to pray for you. Is that okay?"

From that day on, we knew our journey in the United States was going to be saturated by God's presence and the surrounding witness of his people around us.

A week later, we connected with a Nazarene congregation in Cincinnati that ended up being our home church for the two years I attended school. They picked us up and dropped us off every day there was church.

During our first week in Cincinnati we discovered that Rachel was pregnant with our second daughter. We were not ready for that, but we were once again assured that God was going to journey with us through every circumstance. So, on a spring morning in 1991, the Lord graced our home with the birth of our second daughter, Elizabeth. Given all the healing and hope that she meant for us when she was born, we should probably have named her Grace.

Our church in Cincinnati became our family away from home. They loved us as their own. They loved our daughters and surrounded them with affection, gifts, and love. In spite of our severe limitations and trials, the church was again an oasis in the dryness of our life in the United States—but we were ready to leave this particular wilderness phase of our journey.

One day near the end of my schooling, after Sunday service, our pastor noticed the lack of spark in my eyes and asked to talk to me. He told me he was planning to come to our house on Wednesday so we could talk. Dr. Ron Dalton was our pastor. I believe God placed Ron in that church for our time in Cincinnati. A gifted preacher and theologian, Ron had the heart of a pastor and the sensitivity to see God at work in people's lives.

That Wednesday Ron came to our house. He heard about my internal struggles trying to discern why God had taken us out of our homeland just to come to the United States for a degree I didn't think I would use and an education that would help but that I could have gotten without leaving home.

"God is calling you to serve him," Ron said with pastoral certainty.

I jumped off my seat and told Ron that if God were interested in calling me, he would certainly have done that while I was in Guatemala, serving in a church that loved me and had seen me grow in the Lord.

"I don't specialize in the mind of God," he said, "but it is evident to me that all these months the Lord has been calling you and you have just been struggling to accept the call."

He prayed for me and left with me a copy of Dr. Earl Lee's *The Cycle of Victorious Living*. Ron's words, rather than reassuring me, left me even more confused.

It was early 1992, and we were already planning to return to Guatemala, this time with a fourth member added to the family, and a degree I planned to use teaching at my alma mater and working for an international development agency. We were doing all kinds of work in order to secure the funds for our return tickets, and we could see the light at the end of the tunnel—until one Sunday.

It was a crisp and cold Sunday in January of 1992. It had been several weeks since Pastor Ron had told me that my struggles were because I was trying to ignore God's call on my life. I had certainly tried to ignore Ron's words and live my life as if nothing had transpired. On that Sunday, in the middle of Ron's sermon, I felt compelled by God's Spirit to come forward, surrender everything, consecrate everything, and yield to God's will and calling in my life. At that altar on a cold morning in January, God's Holy Spirit took complete control of my life, sanctified me, and sealed me for service. The load had been lifted!

After the service, Ron came to talk to me. "Are you still having problems with your English?" he joked.

"Yes, why?" I answered honestly.

"Well, I was in the middle of the sermon, and I had not even made an altar call when you came forward and knelt for several minutes," he said.

"Well, Pastor," I said, "I wasn't really listening to your sermon. I have been talking to the Lord for a while, and I came to the altar to tell him that I give up—I surrender everything."

I had finally said yes to both the call and the prompting to consecrate everything to God. God was ready for me.

Interestingly, even though I had said yes to the Lord's calling, I didn't know what that meant yet. I just said yes and yielded my will to his plans and desires.

A couple weeks later, I was invited by my good friend Jeff Jakobitz—who was a former missionary to Guatemala—to go to Kansas City, Missouri, and teach as a guest lecturer in the missions program he was leading while on furlough from his missionary assignment. I accepted the invitation, especially because the Fulbright commission would fund the travel and boarding expenses while I finished my master's in community planning with an emphasis on international development.

During that week in February 1992 I met Dr. Steve Weber. I knew of Steve because of my volunteer work as an architect in Guatemala, where my firm partner and I had designed and built dozens of church buildings pro bono, including the Hogar del Niño. The

Hogar was an orphanage in Guatemala sponsored by Nazarene Compassionate Ministries, and we had heard Steve's name during the dedication ceremonies for the new buildings.

My meeting with Steve was a brief one over lunch. Steve was inquisitive and curious about my experience and training. He asked me questions about church-based social transformation, and I, fresh from my recent graduate studies and still rejoicing over the work done in Guatemala, responded with much freedom, not knowing the meeting was serving as a job interview. At the end of the lunch, Steve asked me if I wanted to serve as the global leadership trainer for Nazarene Compassionate Ministries based out of Guatemala. I called to consult with Rachel.

Her response was the same one that she has always given me when the Lord has called us to do something: "If it is from the Lord, we must follow."

By the first week of April, exactly nine years after my conversion, I was beginning the journey of full-time service for the Lord. It had taken me a while, and I almost missed the call, but I am glad that I didn't.

Calling and Vocation in the Twenty-First Century

One of the realities of ministry in Western societies is that, as congregations are growing smaller in size and older in age, fewer people are being called, nurtured, and developed as ministers. In fact, "today's inheritors of the Great Commission are not signing up for vocations in Christian service at anywhere near the rate of their immediate predecessors. This alarming trend—coupled with aggressive evangelization by other world religions" in the West—creates a compounded crisis of vocation in the once rich ministry farm of the world.[1]

---

1. Woodrow Kroll, *The Vanishing Ministry in the 21st Century: Calling a New Generation to Lifetime Service* (Grand Rapids: Kregel Publications, 2002),

To aggravate matters, the thinning population of believers who attend church focus their time on feeding their own spiritual needs while separating the call to full-life discipleship from their personal spiritual quests. In other words, the already limited pool of people being called to ministry is reduced by a paradigm of ministry that was designed more for the twentieth century than for this generation.

A 2014 study on vocation and ministry reported that three-quarters of all adults in the United States express their desire to live meaningful lives, yet only 40 percent of all practicing Christians in the country say they have a clear sense of God's calling on their lives, most of which is not expressed in ministry as we know it.[2] Of these, younger Christians feel the greatest need to be guided and encouraged for ministry. This calls for a review not only of the way the church fosters the calling of believers to ministry but also of the understanding of ministry and vocational service. The church needs to recognize that our call is to be disciples and make disciples, not to be customers who train consumers of the gospel. When we emphasize God's calling to all people to be disciples, ministers, and disciple-makers, entering the vocation for full-time service seems natural.

With this emphasis on the priesthood of all believers in mind, the church also needs to recognize that the types of ministry that gave rise to the modern church in the last couple of centuries may need to change according to the realities of a changed world. In a time of technological advances, global networking, and the polarization of the world, the church needs to identify means of ministry engagement for all people, in all generations, in all locations, so that everyone can fulfill God's calling upon their lives.

---

back cover.

2. The Barna Group, "Three Major Faith and Culture Trends for 2014," February 4, 2014, https://www.barna.com/research/three-major-faith-and-culture-trends-for-2014/.

What Does the Bible Say?

The story of the calling of Samuel reminds us of the reality of calling in dry times. The Bible tells us that, during Samuel's young years, the people of God experienced a deep state of dryness manifested in two evident things: the scarcity of the word of God and of visions (1 Samuel 3:1). Unfortunately, these conditions are also true of modern societies afflicted with spiritual dryness—even in the midst of economic affluence and prosperity. Just like during Samuel's time, societies today are experiencing the endemic scarcity of the Word of God. Such a state of dryness also affects the vision of God's people, even those who serve him. Eli, the priest in charge of God's temple when Samuel was young, was indeed affected by lack of vision. The biblical account tells us that there were at least three areas in which dryness affected even a servant of God.

First, spiritual dryness in the land was so evident that Eli himself had lost his physical sense of vision. The narrative that "Eli, whose eyes were becoming so weak that he could barely see" (v. 2) is the metaphor for Israel's loss of prophetic vision. Eli could barely see and was doing the same things he always did. In times of spiritual dryness, ministers often lack vision and rely on doing only the things they have always done, which become a matter of tradition rather than of calling.

Second, spiritual dryness affects ministers when we spend our time doing ministry without introducing Christ to those under our care. Verse 7 introduces a sad indictment on Eli's work as a minister: "Now Samuel did not yet know the LORD: The word of the LORD had not yet been revealed to him." How ironic! Samuel had been taken to the temple by his mother as a fulfillment of her promise to give her first child to the Lord for his service. Samuel had been under Eli's tutelage for more than a decade, and Eli had introduced him to the tasks of ministry but never to the *reason* for ministry. Eli was so committed to doing the job that he forgot the essence of ministry, which is to introduce others to the grace and love of the Lord. I wonder how many ministers have engaged the services of volunteers, young and old, and have even given them ministry tasks, without exposing them to the depths of the saving and sanctifying love of Christ that can transform their lives. I venture to say there are people ministering in some congregations mainly because of their talents and not because of their testimony of the presence of God in them.

Third, and more convicting, spiritual dryness blinds ministers to the fact that God continues to call people, and we can miss it when he calls those under our care. The biblical narrative tells us that God was clearly calling Samuel, and since Samuel did not yet know God, he approached his mentor for guidance. Sadly, his mentor also missed it the first couple of times (vv. 4–8). Fortunately for Samuel, the power of God's calling is such that it resurfaces even when we are affected by spiritual dryness, and it did so in Eli's heart. He remembered the power of God's calling and told Samuel about it, saving Samuel's ministry (v. 9–10). What a wonderful reality it is to know that God's calling is powerful to keep us going even in the midst of dryness.

God's divine grace put Ron Dalton in my life. His sensitivity to God's Spirit allowed him to sense that God was calling me to full-time ministry, even when I had not gotten the message yet. I almost missed the call because I didn't recognize it. Nevertheless, God provided me with the guidance of a pastor who did not allow spiritual dryness to impact his sensitivity to the voice of God calling those under his care to ministry service.

12

ALMOST LOOKED BACK

WHILE OUR ORIGINAL PLANS were to return to Guatemala in 1992 to resume my teaching position and work in my newly enhanced profession, the reality is that we returned to Guatemala with an entirely different, God-designed plan. My contract with Nazarene Compassionate Ministries assigned me to work out of my office in Guatemala while providing training on church-based social transformation to the six world regions of the denomination. We arrived in Guatemala on March 22, 1992, our sixth wedding anniversary. We were looking forward to our new life of global ministry based in our home country.

But God had a different plan. My first training assignment was in Quito, Ecuador, where the regional office for South America was located. It was the first week of April, and they had organized the first regional conference on compassionate ministries. I had been assigned as the main speaker and trainer, and this was my first test of the new ministry assignment. Steve Weber and his team traveled from Kansas City to meet me there and introduce me to Louie Bustle, the regional director for the denomination in South America.

The conference went well, and we were excited to see that—in spite of the decades-old tensions between the social gospel and prosperity gospel factions in Latin America—South American Nazarenes were open and willing to engage in holistic ministry as an expression of God's love for creation. We had a good number of participants who signed up for the next level of training, and we celebrated that compassionate ministries were taking off in South America.

Upon the return flight from Ecuador, where connecting flights in Miami would take me back to Guatemala and Steve back to Kansas City, Steve asked me to sit by him on the plane because he needed to debrief the results of my first training conference in my new role. To my surprise, he told me that Louie had liked what he saw in our ministry approach and wanted me to move to Ecuador and to do the same job I had been hired to do out of Guatemala. What a shock! Rachel and I had just arrived back in Guatemala after two hard years away, and we hadn't even finished unpacking. Now they were asking us to move our family again.

"I need to talk to my wife" was my natural answer. I knew that our time in the United States had taught us difficult lessons on humility and full dependence on God, and we were still healing from the scars of many of those lessons. We had both been eager to return to our homeland and be with our family and friends, and to have our daughters grow up surrounded by their own people and culture.

So I was hoping Rachel would tell me what I was already thinking: "These two guys are crazy, and neither of them has really known us long enough or well enough to hire us in the first place!" Who would trust someone they'd met only as briefly as these two men had known me? I now believe the Holy Spirit gives people discernment even when our human methods of recruitment fall short.

On our layover in Miami, Steve allowed me to use his calling card to phone Rachel from the airport. He needed an answer right away! I thought this was a positive in making the case to decline the offer because we did not normally make rushed decisions without consulting each other and God in prayer. Pressure was a way out.

When Rachel picked up the phone, we talked briefly about the girls and the conference, and I laid on her the news. "Can you believe these two crazy guys? We haven't even gotten settled in Guatemala, and now they want us to move everything and shift our plans again and move to Ecuador!"

I waited for her response, even though I already knew what it would be because I had rehearsed it in my mind.

"If God is calling, let's go" was her faithful and hopeful response.[1]

My heart sank. I paused and prayed for a moment as I went to talk to Steve.

"I guess we are going to Ecuador," I told Steve when I reached him.

We moved to Quito, Ecuador, in September of that year. From there, the Lord allowed me to help the Church of the Nazarene enter at least six new world areas by providing my knowledge in relief and development. We worked as part of Louie's team in South Amer-

---

1. This story has been recorded in the article by Diana Burch: "If God Is Calling, Let's Go," in the Spring 1995 issue of *World Mission Magazine*.

ica, and I saw God's hand blessing a movement of people in those countries where the transformational message of personal and social holiness was preached and modeled. I was blessed to help train the church in those world areas so they would holistically integrate the proclamation and demonstration of the gospel. By the time I ended my first two years as a missionary, the Lord had allowed me to provide training and consulting services in more than fifty countries on six continents.

In 1994, Louie was elected director of World Missions for the Church of the Nazarene, and he invited me to join him to be part of his strategic mission team in Kansas City. He wanted me to apply the same concepts we had implemented in South America to the rest of the world by helping the church focus on compassionate evangelism. The invitation to return to the United States, however, needed to be affirmed by the Lord. We didn't want to return just to return. We needed to make sure it was God's plan for our lives. This decision, however, had already been affirmed by a personal epiphany in Jordan.

In April of 1993, I was in Jordan assisting local churches in becoming organized to respond to the refugee crisis resulting from the first Gulf War. I had gone to provide technical training for our newly formed ministry to refugees, and I was struggling with the long-term nature of my calling. I knew God had called me and that I was supposed to serve him, but I had also been approached by other ministries and international organizations to apply my knowledge working for them. So, while visiting Mount Nebo with my Jordanian friend Afeef, I went alone to the top of the mountain and had a conversation with the Lord. I asked about his decision not to allow Moses to enter the promised land while there had been many other leaders who had done worse than Moses yet had been allowed full restoration. What did Moses do that prevented his entry?

As I paused in silence, I pictured my life up to that moment. For most of my life, I had been able to set goals, achieve them, forget about them, and fix my eyes on a different goal. I sensed the Lord telling me that the notion of a geographical promised land is limited to an individual's personal ministry and career goals. I imagined God showing Moses a crisp view of the promised land across the Jordan River and telling him that this was what he had been searching for most of his adult life. I then pictured God showing Moses the true promised land—the eternal promise, the land of the never-ending promise. I saw Moses looking at the gift and promise of an eternal home, and then I realized that there is no earthly goal, no earthly promise, and no earthly accomplishment that would ever compare to the gift and glory of "things above, where Christ is, seated at the right hand of God" (Colossians 3:1).

The memory of that Mount Nebo experience has been important in my journey of ministry and service. I have referred to it many times when I have been questioned about (or when I have questioned) my calling and vocation. On those occasions, I have been reminded that I have been called by the Lord to accomplish the mission of his kingdom, for his glory and honor.

The first test of that lesson came weeks after I returned to Ecuador from Jordan. Having just graduated as a Fulbright scholar from the University of Cincinnati, I was offered the opportunity to complete doctoral studies in international policy and relations at a prestigious university in the United States. I shared the letter of invitation with one of my missionary colleagues in the region and told him I had decided not to accept the invitation. Unbeknownst to me, he shared my decision with Louie, my boss, and Louie called me to his office.

"I think you should consider this invitation," he said. "Opportunities like this rarely come twice in our lives."

I knew he wanted me on his team and that his advice was heartfelt and targeted toward my personal development. My response was framed by my experience at the top of Mount Nebo. "I have committed to the Lord that I will not let education get in the way of my calling, my ministry, and my learning." I said it with conviction, and Louie was glad to hear it.

Three years later, under providential circumstances, I was notified that Regent University, through the Latin American Leadership Program (LALP), had selected me as its first Latin American Leadership Scholar to be granted full tuition for the doctoral program in organizational leadership, a program that would allow me to continue serving in my ministry role while providing me with academic, professional, and theological tools to continue my ministry. I graduated May 21, 2001, with a PhD in organizational leadership, and by God's grace my research was used to assist Christian organizations and ministries to thrive beyond mere survival for the glory of God. I am glad the Lord helped me keep my eyes on things above.

Ministry Attrition

Recognizing the needs of ministers as they face the stresses, disappointments, and challenges of ministry, the late Dr. H. B. London cited studies of attrition in the United States that reported that more than 1,700 pastors were leaving the ministry each month.[2] These studies also showed that a vast majority of those leaving the ministry did not intend to do so but found continuing the journey of service to be too difficult.

While the numbers may vary across countries and types of ministry, the reality of ministry attrition is evident, and many churches and denominations need to address it. Ministry attrition has hit some of the most resilient groups, including the missionary community. In fact, a 2007 study on missionary retention discovered that even those who had committed their lives to cross-cultural missions—by learning new languages and leaving their countries, families, and careers to fulfill the Great Commission—had experienced

---

2. H. B. London, "Foreword," in David and Lisa Frisbie, *Managing Stress in Ministry* (Kansas City, MO: Beacon Hill Press of Kansas City, 2014), 13.

large attrition numbers and that ministry and missionary attrition is both preventable and unpreventable, expected and surprising, and painful in all circumstances.[3]

Just as the calling of each minister is God-tailored for the realities of each individual, the circumstances of ministry attrition are also unique for each person, yet there are identifiable circumstances for people to shift their focus from full-time, vocational ministry to more secularized means of service. In some cases, the shift could be as simple as giving in to career distractions or other ministry opportunities that take us away from the core to which we committed. In many other circumstances, however, it has to do with the difficulties of ministry and the lack of coping mechanisms to face such difficulties, whether related to stress, exhaustion, depression, or spiritual warfare. Unfortunately, the list of triggers for the decision to quit is exhaustive, and the church has, at times, not developed the proper mechanisms to assist those who are at the brink of renouncing their call to ministry.

Ministers in general leave ministry because of family, financial, health, and interpersonal reasons. Others leave because they have lost motivation or been attracted to other ministry or professional opportunities. However, two of the most common emotional triggers that result in ministry attrition are stress and exhaustion. These two can and should be easily preventable.

What Does the Bible Say?

The narrative of 1 Kings 19 tells us the story of a minister who had been extremely successful in his spiritual battle against the prophets of Baal yet, because of exhaustion, reached the point of what we could call "ministerial euthanasia." Elijah had just been an instrument of God's power as he defeated hundreds of prophets of

---

3. Rob Hay, *Worth Keeping: Global Perspectives on Best Practice in Missionary Retention* (Pasadena: William Carey Library, 2007).

evil. He was victorious, and the power of the Lord was with him (1 Kings 18:46).

However, immediately after such a powerful spiritual victory, Elijah was threatened by Jezebel, an evil woman who promised to take his life. The godly man who defeated hundreds of evil prophets through the power of God was now so afraid that he decided to run for his life. The man who had claimed victory just a few days prior was now so exhausted that he reflected all the stages of attrition: exhaustion, fear, loneliness, low self-esteem, and a desire to quit.

Elijah ran out of energy, and he was exhausted and ready to die (19:4). The fear and exhaustion were compounded by a sense of loneliness and deepening feelings of insecurity and low self-esteem. When an angel of the Lord asked Elijah about his escape, Elijah answered that he was "the only one left" (v. 10) after previously confessing that he was "no better than my ancestors" (v. 4).

Elijah was so exhausted, drained, and depressed that he had reached the point of ministerial euthanasia. He felt so lonely and inadequate that he was not merely willing but actually desirous of being put to death—even though he had run away to avoid death. The paradox of ministerial euthanasia is that we reach a point where we are willing to give up even the most sacred gift of ministry because our minds and hearts are blinded by the pressures of ministry itself.

Fortunately, the one who called us is always there with us, even—and perhaps especially—in times of anguish, fear, exhaustion, and desolation. Just as Elijah collapsed in a deep state of stress-related tiredness, the angel of the Lord appeared to him and reminded him that he—the Angel of the Lord—was there at the point of his crisis to sustain Elijah and accompany him on the journey.

"Get up and eat" were the angel's words (v. 5). The angel of the Lord was the provider of bread and water—in the same way that Jesus described himself in the Gospel of John (John 4:10–14; 6:32–35, 41, 48–51; 7:37–39). "'Get up and eat, for the journey is too much for you.' So he got up and ate and drank. Strengthened by that food, he traveled forty days and forty nights until he reached Horeb, the mountain of God" (1 Kings 19:7–8). The one who called Elijah was with him, both at the point of his crisis and for the extent of his journey. He empathized with him, accompanied him, and strengthened him for the rest of the journey.

Elijah was close to quitting. The man—the prophet who had just experienced an amazing spiritual victory—was ready to quit because he was exhausted. But the Lord was with him. He was there to remind him that he had not called him to the ministry journey by himself. His promise and his company were Elijah's strength. Renewed by God's strength, Elijah was able to finish the journey.

This is also true for many of us who are on the journey of ministry. The reason the narratives of Moses and Elijah—two of the greatest prophets of the Old Testament—are recorded in the Bible as servants who reached the point of ministerial euthanasia is to remind us that none of us is exempt from reaching the point when we may feel tempted to give up. But, even at the lowest points of our ministry journeys, the Lord—the one who called us—is there to pick us up, to feed and sustain us, to journey with us, and to take us safely home, until we finish the journey and reach his presence.

13
ALMOST SELECTED

MY FAMILY AND I left Ecuador for the United States in September of 1994. This time I had been asked to move to Kansas City to work in the development of compassionate ministries globally and to implement the integrational model of leadership development that we had put in place in South America. The Lord helped us again and, by the middle of 1996, we had put in place the infrastructure to mobilize the local church to minister to the poor as part of the witness of God's people. It became apparent that the training, the background, the global exposure, and the work with churches and communities were all put together by God for the service of the church. God blessed our ministry.

Because of the exposure that the Lord and the church allowed me to experience during my initial years in ministry, I was invited as a speaker, trainer, and consultant to many international ministries devoted to mobilizing the church for social ministry and community transformation. In 1997 I was asked to serve as vice president of the Association of Evangelical Relief and Development Organizations of the U.S. (AERDO). Because of this privilege, I was later invited to serve as a field manager for Compassion International, a global Christian child development organization based in Colorado Springs, and later as senior vice president for the World Relief Corporation of the National Association of Evangelicals in the U.S. Between 1999 and 2003, the Lord allowed me to serve the global church as a Nazarene minister committed to mobilizing Christians to serve the poor and the disenfranchised in the name of Jesus.

I again traveled to Jordan in March 2003, ten years after the affirmation of my call at Mount Nebo. This time I was representing the global evangelical alliance of relief ministries that later became Integral Alliance in order to put together the coalition to respond to the plight of refugees and displaced people resulting from the second war in Iraq. On my way to Jordan, I needed to stop in Denmark, where the meeting of the alliance was taking place. The idea was that I would carry the plans for the alliance to organize the evangelical response on the ground in Jordan.

March in Denmark is cold and snowy. I got off the train in the small town of Hellerup and walked to the hotel in the middle of a snowstorm. The streets were empty and cold. When I arrived at the hotel I took a hot shower then decided to go to the hotel restaurant for dinner. I was the only person there when two older ladies arrived. They sat for a few minutes and then left. I was pondering in fascination the snow, the culture, the place, and the few people I'd seen when I heard a voice from the interior of my heart. It was probably my thoughts, but I believe God put them in my heart. *What if I called you to come to Europe to do ministry in my name?* I sat there in shocked silence, wondering if I were experiencing some aftereffects of my cold walk in the snowstorm.

One day, seven months later, I got a phone call from Dr. Bustle, who said to me, "Dr. Franklin Cook, the regional director of the Church of the Nazarene in Eurasia, is retiring next year. Are you willing to let your name stand as one of the potential candidates for the position?" That call on October 3, 2003, changed again the course of my ministry. I hadn't shared with anyone other than Rachel about the inner conversation I'd had in Denmark.

Less than a year later, my family and I moved to Germany, where I served as regional director for the Church of the Nazarene in Eurasia. The transition was not easy because my election was met with resistance from almost every level in the church. I still remember getting a letter from someone I had previously considered a good friend in Eurasia—someone with whom I had worked in social ministries. He told me that for the good of my family, my reputation, and my ministry, the best thing I could do was decline the invitation because Europe was different than Latin America and the U.S., and a Latino didn't have much to contribute to church development in Europe.

Funnily enough, I wholeheartedly agreed with his assessment. The truth is that nobody really has anything to contribute to the kingdom of God, other than a willingness to serve. I told my friend that, while his counsel was received, I couldn't refuse God's calling on me to go wherever and whenever he called.

My decision to accept the invitation was affirmed by the fact that, just two days before I departed for Eurasia on June 1, 2004, I had the sad privilege of attending my mother's funeral. Mom and I had been talking about this invitation, and she encouraged me to follow the Lord's lead "even if you go far away where we may not see each other that often." We had left our home and work in Maryland, and we had said goodbye to our family in Guatemala. We were ready for the next assignment for the Lord.

The first year in Eurasia was not easy. I had numerous meetings with field leaders and their missionaries, many of whom doubted the wisdom of the church in electing me for that important missionary role. I also had meetings with national leaders, and their response was different. They were open to dialogue. They were open to partnering with the mission of the church in reaching the lost in Eurasia. During those trying first months, I remembered the affirmation I had received from the Lord at Mount Nebo, a place I had visited again in March of 2003 to reaffirm my calling to serve God above all else. An emphasis on the calling, listening to the grassroots, and a focus on the mission of God helped me build the team and prayerfully launch the strategy that would help us move forward from being the smallest region in the denomination (67,000 members in 1,100 organized churches) to becoming a movement committed to the mission to "transform the world, in Christ, like Christ, and for Christ."

After my first year as a regional director I had the responsibility to report to the denomination at its General Assembly in Indianapolis, Indiana. It was June of 2005, and I was barely cognizant of the global dynamics of such a vast and diverse denomination—the largest Wesleyan-Arminian denomination in the world. We had traveled to Argentina to attend the funeral of our friend and colleague, Dr. Bruno Radi, who had died just days before the General Assembly while serving as regional director for the church in South America. The world of the Nazarene family had been shaken by this loss, and we weren't prepared for what followed.

The business of the assembly took place as expected, and the church seemed to be ready to elect—for the first time in its history—a general superintendent from outside of North America. After many ballots that resulted in one election and a couple of declinations, something strange happened: my name started climbing in the ballots, and it got scarily close to resulting in my election as a general superintendent. To say I was shocked would be an understatement. I had been serving the global church as a regional director for a little over a year, and I assumed my name appearing on the ballot was perhaps a reaction to Dr. Radi's death, as well as the other declinations that had already happened over the course of the assembly's business.

When the last ballot was read prior to the dinner break, my name was at the top, but fortunately, it was not high enough to declare election by a two-thirds vote of the delegates. I left the meeting hall and called my wife and daughters, who were with me in Indianapolis for the assembly. We called our friends from Guatemala to join us at the "furthest place to eat from the convention center" so we could pray and talk. At that dinner, I asked the Lord to please do something to keep this election from happening. I was too young. My oldest daughter, Raquel, had just graduated from high school, and she was preparing to move to the U.S. to go to college. My youngest, Beth, was just about to start high school, and I needed to be with her during these key formative years of her life. I couldn't be present in her life if I was traveling the world as a general superintendent. We prayed together and asked the Lord to leave that election so I would be considered "almost elected," which was enough of an accomplishment for me.

We returned to the meeting hall that evening, and things changed as expected after dinner. I am told that dinnertimes are when the human side of the church is used by God to adjust things but that, at the end of the day, God ultimately decides according to his will. This is precisely what happened after the thirty-fifth ballot on June 29, 2005. My name disappeared from the ballot results, and Dr. J. K. Warrick was elected as the thirty-sixth general superintendent for the Church of the Nazarene.

However, God used the vote at that General Assembly to help me with an important piece I needed for my leadership in Eurasia: affirmation. I didn't think that I personally needed affirmation, but the Lord saw it fitting for me to return to the region to continue leading the team, and as a result, I discovered that sometimes people need to see others affirm a leader before they decide to follow. I guess that is part of being human.

Encouraged by the support of the global Nazarene family, we returned to Eurasia to become part of an exciting church-planting, church-development, and leadership-development movement. Inspired by the vision of God and empowered by his Spirit, we worked alongside local and district leaders to mobilize the region for holistic growth. The smallest world region in the denomination was now on pace to double its statistics in almost every area. From 64,000 members in 2004, the region nearly doubled to almost 125,000 members. From 1,100 organized churches, the region doubled to more than 2,300. God was at work, and the work of the church was being blessed.

We attended the quadrennial assembly again in 2009. We were ready to report of God's work among his people in Eurasia. There was a feeling of excitement and celebration for what God was doing there. The growth of the church there allowed us to bring a larger number of delegates, who were coming to our global celebration to represent their countries for the first time. It was an exciting gathering.

The memory of the General Assembly in Orlando, Florida, in June 2009 brings me a lot of mixed emotions. During that assembly I received the news that my dad had been taken to the hospital and placed in intensive care because of his terminal kidney disease. We continued with the business of the assembly, but my heart and mind were not there. I was thinking about my dad. Dad had always reminded me that the most important call of a servant was that of obedience and that obedience was not always connected to position, but it *was* always connected to faith.

Three new general superintendents were elected at that General Assembly in 2009. Just like in 2005, my name emerged as a candidate only to experience a sudden spike and even more dramatic dip. My family and I were confident this was God's way of letting us and the church know that my time in Eurasia was not over, that there was still work to do there, and that we needed to be obedient.

My dad passed away exactly one week after the closing of the assembly. On July 10, 2009, we said goodbye to Dad, and I prepared to continue serving in Eurasia. Upon my return to the office, I found a card that a pastor friend from Europe had sent me. It read, "Congratulations on being almost elected general superintendent. We welcome you back to Eurasia, where you are loved and needed." It was the same friend who, five years earlier, had sent me the letter discouraging me from accepting the role of regional director.

The dream to double the region's numbers every four years continued in our hearts and minds, and we worked with a committed team of pastors, district leaders, missionaries, and field leaders with a renewed sense of strategic passion. The Lord of the harvest blessed the work of his people! By the end of 2012, the region was positioned to double again and, this time, to become one of the largest regions of the Church of the Nazarene in terms of membership and organized churches. There was a movement of indigenous leadership development that had raised local leaders, and now we felt from the Lord that we were ready to move on as missionaries who are called to go, train, develop, model, mentor, and move on.

Rachel and I knew that, this time, our work in Eurasia was nearing an end after nearly ten years of ministry. We knew so because, as missionaries, we always did our best to work ourselves out of a job by developing local leaders, and Eurasia had not been the exception. We both received confirmation of that feeling at an event in Guatemala. I had been invited to speak at the National Forum on Poverty Alleviation in Guatemala in August 2012, where there were participants and representatives from the national government, the private sector, the nonprofit sector, and the church. This was my first time back in the public arena in Guatemala since 1992, and I was blessed by the way my own people received the message I brought on behalf of the church of Christ.

At the end of the first conference, I was invited to go to the "green room" to wait for the journalists who were going to interview me for the national media. While I was sitting there, I clearly felt the Lord telling me that the work I had done in Eurasia was finished and that it was time to turn it over to indigenous leadership. I didn't know how to share this with Rachel because it was too clear but too blunt. It would mean another change after ten years. Not surprisingly, though, when Rachel joined me in the green room, she had something to tell me. She said that, while listening to the content of my first speech, she realized we had completed our work in Eurasia! The message was clear, but the next steps were not.

We announced our decision to leave Eurasia to the leadership of the region in October of that year. We felt the Lord calling us to return to the dream of twenty years before, when we had been called to a global assignment to mobilize the church by turning the church over to the next generation. While we felt that this was the right direction, we still were unclear about what next—and how. After the announcement in October, we organized our biannual training meeting with the district superintendents of the Eurasia region for April 2013. The schedule called for a meeting in Jordan, where we had met our leaders in 2007.

There I was, at the top of Mount Nebo again. It had been twenty years since I made there a covenant of lifetime service with the Lord. Twenty years before I'd been by myself, looking at Jerusalem and having an epiphany with the Lord. This time, I was among more than forty district superintendents and missionaries who surrounded Rachel and me and commissioned us for the next phase of our lives.

We attended the twenty-sixth General Assembly in June 2013 with the purpose of meeting the leaders of Nazarene Compassionate Ministries I would be training in the years to come. The older generation of leaders had gone by, and it was time to train and empower the next generation. Everything was ready for the next phase of our lives. We planned to live in Guatemala while training thousands of leaders with the lessons we had learned over twenty years of missionary service.

The planning meeting took place in the afternoon of June 26, 2013. My friends and colleagues from the team had prepared for me a beautiful welcome cake that read: "Congratulations! 567=NCM Wins!" This was not a coded message. It meant that, at the business sessions of the assembly the two prior days, my name had been in the ballots in the same way as 2005 and 2009. I had almost been elected once again but fell short of the required number of votes at 567. Therefore, Nazarene Compassionate Ministries (NCM) was ready for me, and I was ready to continue the work I had started with them twenty years earlier.

But God had a different plan, another vote occurred, and this is what the World Methodist Council reported in their July 2013 newsletter about how events played out that afternoon and evening:

Gustavo A. Crocker, Eurasia regional director, was elected the 41st general superintendent of the Church of the Nazarene Wednesday, June 26. He was elected on the 53rd ballot at the 28th General Assembly in Indianapolis, Indiana.

"Your vote is a demonstration that grace exists," Crocker said after arriving at the podium. . . .

The 53 ballots it took to elect Crocker is a record in the Church of the Nazarene, surpassing the 51 ballots it took to elect Stan Toler in 2009.

After ballot 46, Olivet Nazarene University President John Bowling suggested that delegates do three things: 1. Step across the aisle to get to know someone to help promote unity, which he felt was fading; 2. Kneel in prayer; 3. Hit the "restart button" on voting intentions, trying to reestablish authenticity if it was missing. The chair agreed and, after the prayer, a feeling of Spirit-given peace filled the room. . . .

Prayer was not limited to the Indiana Convention Center as many following the proceedings on Twitter and 1,900 watching on nazarene.org knelt in prayer too. Tweets began pouring in with

Nazarenes saying what state or country they were from and that they were praying. Crocker was elected shortly thereafter. . . .

After asking the assembly to pray for him, he confessed that earlier he thought about what his answer would be if he were elected.

"It was not until tonight as we went on our knees that both my wife and I—sitting on different sides of this auditorium—received the same message from the Lord: 'Give it all and serve all for me.'"[1]

Rachel and I knew that the Lord had spoken to both of us. This has been the way he has let us know of most of his decisions for our lives. He has made it clear for both of us that we are one and that this journey with him is for the two of us. Together.

We don't know how long the Lord wants me to serve in this humbling assignment on behalf of his church, an assignment I accepted gratefully in 2013 and still have as of 2021. We don't need to know how long, though. God already knows. When I agreed to serve as regional director in Eurasia against all odds, a friend of mine asked me if I was worried about failing. I answered, "Failure is to be outside of the will of God. As long as you are obedient to his will, even when you don't meet the human metrics or standards, you are still successful." This was my answer then, and it remains my answer today.

The Secularization of the Sacred and the Spiritualization of the Secular

The modern history of humanity has been marked by increased confusion between secular and sacred matters, particularly when it comes to public policy and political choice. Unfortunately, that confusion has been fueled by the historical fact that, for centuries,

---

1. World Methodist Council, "Church of the Nazarene Elects New General Superintendents," First Friday Letter, July 2013, www.firstfridayletter.world methodistcouncil.org.

church and state have operated in adjacent positions of power—if not merged entirely. With the establishment of Christianity as the state religion of the Byzantine Empire ruled by Constantine, the line between secular and sacred was forever blurred. This model has been carried for generations of the expansion of Christianity in the world.

This secularization of the sacred has made it look normal when the church and its members engage in and apply methods of secular policy analysis and political reason to involve the church in the daily affairs of society. In fact, in their study of religion and post-secularism, Samantha May and her co-authors affirm that "the intertwining of politics and religion is not a new phenomenon."[2] They go so far as to suggest, through a historical analysis of the mutual impact of religion and politics, that religious and political systems are intermingled rituals that are part of community life. Unfortunately, this historical blurring of the line between the sacred and the secular has caused the church to embrace (and at times promote) secular models of policy and political engagement in the sacred institutions of the church itself.

While we cannot separate the fact that, as humans, we are part of societies that are impacted by policies developed through political reasoning and action, we need to distinguish our role as living actors in two worlds. On one hand, we are called to participate in seeking the peace and prosperity of the communities where the Lord has planted us through civic engagement and political responsibility. On the other hand, we need to ensure that the secular means of policy and politics do not permeate the sacred life and means of grace of the church as God's instrument to carry out his mission of reconciliation.

---

2. Samantha May, Erin K. Wilson, Claudia Baumgart-Ochse, and Faiz Sheikh, "The Religious as Political and the Political as Religious: Globalisation, Post-Secularism and the Shifting Boundaries of the Sacred," *Politics, Religion & Ideology* 15:3 (2014), 331–46.

What Does the Bible Say?

King Saul was an example of the tension of living between the sacred and the secular. As king, he represented the secular desire of God's people to have a ruler of the same standards and office as other kingdoms. God allowed them to have a king with the understanding that this was satisfying a secular desire. However, God did not compromise or dismiss the value of the sacred, which was intended to remain sacred.

The story of King Saul as narrated in 1 Samuel illustrates the challenges of secularizing the sacred and spiritualizing the secular. Saul was expected to wait for the spiritual leader to present the burnt offering to God while waiting in Gilgal (1 Samuel 10:8). He was responsible for the strategic part of the assignment, and Samuel had been assigned the spiritual part of it. Later, thinking that the secret to military victory was a spiritual ritual, Saul assumed the role of spiritual leadership and decided to secularize the sacred (see 1 Samuel 13). He assumed that by doing things spiritually, he had cared for the strategic dimension of the battle. Samuel evaluated Saul's actions clearly: "You have done a foolish thing" (v. 13).

This was not Saul's last foolish action. According to the narrative of 1 Samuel 15, this time God did give Saul a spiritual assignment disguised as a strategic battle. Saul was supposed to carry out God's instructions to cleanse the kingdom from impure sacrifices, including all animals, but Saul made a calculated choice. He decided to keep as plunder the best animals of those he had subdued. He turned a spiritual command into a pragmatic, secular process of conquest. It is no wonder that in a second encounter with Samuel, Saul was rebuked again (15:10–23).

Throughout centuries, one of the biggest difficulties for God's people has been the ability to distinguish between the secular and the sacred, particularly when they intermingle in our daily lives. We have, at times, used the means of the world in the sacred practices of the church, and we have been unable to give to Caesar what belongs to Caesar and to God what belongs to God (see Matthew 22:21; Mark 12:17; Luke 20:25).

Once God rejected Saul as Israel's king, the prophet Samuel had an important task to accomplish. Now that Saul was deemed unfit to rule God's people, it was time to choose his successor. Samuel—the same one who advocated before the Lord not to let the people have a king (see 1 Samuel 8)—was now in charge of selecting the new king. His instructions were clear, and the process was outlined for him (1 Samuel 16). He went to Bethlehem as he was told and met the people there. He made sure the people of God knew this was a spiritual process, and he invited them to consecrate themselves and join him in the anointing ritual of leadership selection (16:5).

However, as the sons of Jesse were presented, Samuel learned one of the deepest lessons in selecting servant leaders: that the patterns of leadership selection among God's people are often influenced by the patterns of this world rather than by God's design. The people of Israel had already shown such inclination by demanding to have a king like the other nations even though they knew that the Lord was their king (12:12). And now, influenced by the patterns of the time, Samuel, God's chosen prophet, was using the same means to select the new king (albeit in the midst of a spiritual exercise).

When Samuel saw the children of Jesse, he used the normal human patterns of leadership selection. He reviewed their appearance, their stature, their command, their presence. He wanted to make sure these candidates met the standards set by the other nations in bringing forth a king. But God corrected Samuel's secular approach to leadership selection: "Do not consider his appearance or his height, for I have rejected him. The LORD does not look at the things people look at. People look at the outward appearance, but the LORD looks at the heart" (16:7).

The influence of secular thinking had permeated even the mind of God's prophet. He had become familiarized with the polity of the time and was ready to apply these human methods to inform the spiritual process. We cannot blame Samuel. He was surely working on the basis of consecration and sacrifice, and he didn't see a problem with applying secular standards to a divine assignment. The king was a secular role anyway.

However, God's lesson for Samuel, for God's people, and for us today is that we cannot afford to compromise the sacred by intermingling it with the secular. While we can use institutional mechanisms and processes that would help us identify, develop, train, and release servant leaders in God's kingdom, the selection process for any and all who are called to lead the church must be bathed in prayer and ratified by the Holy Spirit while considering the eternal kingdom values that must shape the anointing of servants.

I do not claim that my election to office was the only true spiritual exercise in our polity. On the contrary, when I look at the list of servant leaders who have preceded me in office and listen to their wonderful testimonies of service, piety, and commitment to the Lord, I am humbled to recognize that, if I have had the privilege to serve in this and other humbling capacities in the church of Christ, it is because it has been pleasing to God and anointed by his Holy Spirit.

I pray that the church—that divine institution comprising imperfect humans—will always be able to discern and comprehend the spiritual dimension of its calling and that, as the bride of Christ, she will be able to focus on the matters that matter—the things of the kingdom of God. I also pray that, in doing so, the church will be able to remain pure and spotless, unpolluted by society and the world. Let it be so.

14
ALWAYS LOVED

IT WAS A SPRINGLIKE AFTERNOON in Guatemala in December 2010. My older brother and I had decided to travel to the north of the country to visit some of the places we had grown up. Since he is ten years older than me and his memories and experiences with the civil war and family life were different than mine, we decided to write a biographical account of our parallel journeys with and for the poor. The narrative of our stories is part of a different writing project.

As we reviewed our stories, I had the ignorant audacity to tell my brother that, in spite of all the circumstances I had lived, I didn't have any major scars I could remember, no trauma so ingrained in my memory that I had not been able to overcome it.

"I guess I grew up with much resilience," I told him arrogantly.

His answer is what encouraged me to write this book: "It is not that you are exceptionally resilient. What happened to you is that, whether it was because you were a sickly child or because you were the youngest, or because you always looked vulnerable, the entire family always loved you and took extra care to protect you."

That's it! Love is the answer. It has always been. It will always be. Love has the power to help us endure any difficulty, obstacle, disability, or circumstance. Love gives an average underdog the power to overcome. Love is the answer!

When I was not worth carrying to term, my mother loved me from the depths of her womb.

When I was supposed to be left for dead, my mother and my father loved me into life.

When I was nearly blind, my family loved me and gave me light.

When I was poor, the love of my family made me feel rich.

When I was condemned by a legalist, the love of a believer brought me to Jesus.

When I was afraid after my brother's death, love carried the family through.

When I was forgotten, I was loved into the fellowship of the church.

When I was lonely, God brought me to my companion to share a life full of love.

When I was rejected, others loved me into God's plans.

When I was about to give up, the love of Christ compelled me.

When I was not chosen, the church showed me a love that transcends politics.

In all of those circumstances, the love of God was ever-present!

My life is not a special story written for a special individual. My life is the story of an average underdog. Perhaps the only difference is that, in spite of myself, I have allowed love to permeate my life, even when I didn't deserve it or even know it was happening.

A Love Poem Based on 1 Corinthians 13

I am nothing.

I can communicate with eloquence and even preach
the Word of God.
But if I do it without genuine love, I am nothing!

I can understand the times and speak with knowledge and authority. I can be the best-educated professional and scientist. I can even have supernatural powers to move mountains.
But if I do it without genuine love, I am nothing!

I can become a martyr on behalf of the poor, the needy, and the marginalized. I can be an activist for the sake of those who suffer and the disenfranchised.
But if I do it without genuine love, I am nothing!

My ministry, my knowledge, my passion, my gifting,
even my endeavors on behalf of others—
All are meaningless unless they are born out of the genuine,
sacrificial, unselfish, true love of God residing in me.

This is how we recognize genuine love:
it is willing to wait beyond our reason;
it is willing to suffer beyond our comprehension;
it is ready to show kindness when others don't deserve it;
it considers others better than ourselves;
it is humble to the point of renouncing our right to defend ourselves;
it concedes victory to others;
it seeks peace and reconciliation at all costs;
it is faithful, truthful, hopeful, respectful;
it is eternal and infallible, enduring, assuring.

Other things will cease even when we place them
at the top of our lists.
But love will always be.
Love is always the answer.

Always loved, always thankful,
Gustavo Crocker